"In *Satan Fears You'll Discover Your True Identity*, Kraft assists Christians in understanding and living out their true identity in Christ, and he does so in a way that is both readable and in-depth. Sometimes provocative yet biblically based, this book obviously grows out of a lifetime of study and decades of experience in deep-level healing. I recommend it!"

Thomas J. Sappington, Th.D., associate professor of intercultural studies, Cook School of Intercultural Studies; chair, Department of Missions and Intercultural Studies, Talbot School of Theology, Biola University

"The identity and authority of Christ followers, the age-old conflict between Christ followers and powers of darkness, and the importance of inner healing prayer for increased spiritual freedom are key life messages of Charles Kraft that he skillfully brings together in this short yet powerful book. I highly recommend it!"

John Jay Travis, Ph.D., affiliate professor of intercultural studies and spiritual dynamics, Fuller Theological Seminary

SATAN
FEARS YOU'LL
DISCOVER
YOUR TRUE
IDENTITY

Books by Charles H. Kraft

SATAN
FEARS YOU'LL
DISCOVER
YOUR TRUE
IDENTITY

DO YOU KNOW *who* YOU ARE?

CHARLES H. KRAFT

Chosen

a division of Baker Publishing Group
Minneapolis, Minnesota

© 2019 by Charles H. Kraft

Published by Chosen Books
11400 Hampshire Avenue South
Bloomington, Minnesota 55438
www.chosenbooks.com

Chosen Books is a division of
Baker Publishing Group, Grand Rapids, Michigan

Printed in the United States of America

ISBN 978-0-8007-9929-8

Library of Congress Cataloging-in-Publication Control Number: 2018043801

The information given in *Satan Fears You'll Discover Your True Identity* is biblical, pastoral and spiritual in nature. It is not professional counsel and should not be viewed as such. The names and other identifying details of certain individuals have been changed to protect their privacy.

Cover design by Greg Jackson, Thinkpen Design, Inc.

19 20 21 22 23 24 25   7 6 5 4 3 2 1

green press INITIATIVE

Contents

Contents

Foreword

Several decades ago, I started my first appointment to full-time ministry. My wife and I had just graduated from Bible school and college, and our eyes had been set on going to the mission field. But since our mission felt we needed some ministry experience, we approached my home church, which appointed me as assistant to the pastor. My duties included praying for the sick and visiting new members.

I still remember those old days and the anemic prayers I offered on behalf of the sick. The best I could do was ask God to guide the hands of the physicians and to speed up the sick person's recovery, if healing was within His will. I was afraid to be too aggressive in asking for healing because if healing did not come, then I was putting God into an embarrassing situation. Even worse, I was embarrassing myself by my lack of effective praying. So couching my anemic prayers in conditions that put the authority back into the hands of God and His will gave God an out, thereby saving us both from powerlessness.

It would be two decades before I came to realize that God does not like to see His children in pain, and that He has given us authority already to claim His power. He wants to bring healing and forgiveness to those who are in pain. But I had not yet learned to exercise my identity as God's representative on behalf of those who are servants of sin, who are broken in body and crushed by damaged emotions—and I did not know how to pray for them.

Unfortunately, countless others shared my impotence in prayer, and so we fumbled along. But the Holy Spirit was about to begin a new work among His people.

Slowly at first, a few brave souls began to experiment with taking God at His word by starting to pray with authority on behalf of His people. Among those with the courage to face their own ignorance and fear: Dr. Charles Kraft.

Fortunately, Dr. Kraft was brave and skilled enough as a writer to share his journey in print. And for more than thirty years now, he has shared his experiences, his insights from the Word of God and his emerging strategies in praying for the people the Scriptures refer to sometimes as the "brokenhearted." In the course of his many books on the topic of spiritual warfare, Dr. Kraft has advocated a return to the biblical practices of praying for the sick, setting the captives free and claiming our authority in Christ.

In this new book, Dr. Kraft shares from his years of experience in bringing healing to people with painful memories of past abuse. This is not a combative book in which he seeks to answer his critics or defend his practices. It reflects the very best of the pastoral side of Dr. Kraft as he affirms for believers the multiple ways God has provided for us as His sons and daughters—co-laborers in the struggle against the ravages of sin and heirs of His promises.

Dr. Kraft also identifies the multiple ways Satan seeks to destroy our confidence in God's promises and provisions. He challenges us from the very first chapter to discover and recover our true identity in Christ. In each succeeding chapter, Dr. Kraft identifies specific ways Satan seeks to overwhelm believers with lies, damaged emotions, ugly memories and bad experiences that leave us feeling powerless and helpless.

Then, into every one of these settings, Dr. Kraft gently shares God's provisions for our healing, using inner healing strategies that move beyond simply knowing a truth to experiencing it at the deeper level of our hearts and memories.

One of his techniques for inner healing is faith picturing, a technique he has developed and used over the years to bring healing to countless people in pain. The beauty of this approach is that it departs from an older approach used by many Christian counselors and ministers that tried to heal people by bombarding them with more knowledge. While knowledge and truth are indeed essential steps in our healing process, even more needed is the ability to get that truth from our heads down into our hearts and into the seat of our emotions.

This became evident to me some time ago when I stopped to reflect on a favorite image of mine. In my mind I love to reflect on some point in the future when I can walk along the banks of the River of Life with Jesus by my side, and we are chatting, and I can ask all the questions I want. This has been my visualization of being fully accepted by

God the Son, my best Friend and Savior. Lacking in this picture, however, is a place for God the Father.

Frankly, I have always had a difficult time calling God the Father *Abba* or *Daddy*. My own father was a distant, harsh man, and I have no real memories of doing anything fun with him.

One day at one of his conferences, Dr. Kraft asked us to picture sitting on the lap of God the Father. I found myself struggling with that picture. In fact, I was blocked emotionally from envisioning God as my Father. As I struggled with this realization, I became aware that while I understood God intellectually to be my Father, I was still unable emotionally to appropriate it.

That was when I decided to create a new mental picture, one that would speak to my needs. So I returned to my picture of walking along the banks of the River of Life with Jesus by my side. But this time I pictured myself as being on a picnic by the River of Life with both Jesus and the Father sitting with me. We are able to talk about the creation and my place in it and the plans that both Jesus and the Father have for me in the days ahead. In this scenario I am not the forgotten child but part of God's plan for the universe. And with this love and acceptance, I find a fresh path toward acknowledging who I am as a child of the heavenly Father.

The goal of such mental imaging is not the creation of some form of fantasy world; rather, it is an attempt to use pictures to better understand the spiritual realities of God's promises to us. The practice of mental imaging may seem strange, even uncomfortable at first. But I have found it a powerful tool for breaking through emotional barriers toward newfound freedom in Christ.

I encourage you, therefore, to appropriate the truths about who you are in Christ, to engage with these stories from a master prayer counselor and to experiment with visualizing Christ as walking with you toward a fuller healing from the sin and brokenness of the past.

Douglas Hayward, Ph.D., professor emeritus, anthropology and intercultural studies, Biola University

Acknowledgments

I want to specially acknowledge my Baker editors Ann Weinheimer and Jane Campbell for the important part they have played in making this book what it has become. I thank Ann especially for going well beyond what her job required to reduce repetition and to improve the organization and the flow. I bless and thank both of you.

Introduction

Our enemy, Satan, is afraid of us. He knows that we are on God's side with access to all of God's power. We "out-power" him. So if he is to defeat us, it will have to be through deceit and bluff.

When I pray with people for inner healing, I will sometimes encounter a demonic presence that speaks to me through the person being prayed for. On one occasion, a demon asked me, "Where did you get this power?" I guess he thought I had some power of my own. This I denied. As soon as I mentioned that I was in partnership with Jesus, however, he had his answer. The demon knew right away that he was finished if I knew what he knew about who Jesus is. I knew and I won.

There is a battle in the human context over whether or not we are important and, if we are, what that means. Many see humans as simply high animals. Is this all we are? What does our existence mean to God, what does it mean to us and what does it mean to Satan?

These are the issues I seek to discuss in this book; I have noticed that our enemy, Satan, seems to be winning the battle over whether or not we are allowed to feel good about who we are. The fact that we fail a lot bothers us and supports our tendency to put ourselves down. Holding a low opinion of ourselves is often mistaken for humility. Our sinfulness is often considered the norm. Failure to live up to God's standards is expected. And Satan wins.

If we are so bad and unable to please God, how come He has not given up on us? Does He value something here so much that He refuses to give up on us? I believe so.

The enemy knows who we are and what our relationship with God implies. But most of us ignore the fact that we, in partnership with God, carry infinitely more power than does our enemy.

Satan is often portrayed as very powerful. But most of his power is given to him by humans. When humans sin, they partner with Satan, handing him power. This is what happened in the Garden when Adam, on behalf of all his descendants, partnered with Satan. In disobeying God, Adam empowered Satan.

At the human level, the issue was disobedience. At the spiritual level, the issue was partnership. And the two interact. Disobedience to God automatically empowers Satan. Obedience to God automatically "empowers" God—*for everything works on two levels simultaneously.* Things that happen on the human level have a counterpart on the spiritual level. Things that happen on the spiritual level have a counterpart on the human level.

The early chapters of this book deal with what is called "self-image"—what we think of ourselves. This is a human-level issue involving how we see ourselves. Those chapters, though, also show a spiritual counterpart that we might call "spiritual-image"—how God and the spirit world see us.

From that start we move to a consideration of the special things about us that make up who we really are in spiritual eyes as well as in human eyes. We want to see ourselves as we are seen from God's perspective as well as Satan's.

These insights, then, inform us as to how we should behave, based on who we really are in contrast with who the enemy says we are. God's people have more power at their disposal than the enemy has at his. We should learn to behave as who we really are, rather than exist in fear.

In partnership with Jesus we discover our true identity, and we win.

EXERCISE

To drive this truth home, let's do an exercise. Find a mirror, preferably a full-length mirror. Look into it and note how you feel. When I started doing this, my first feelings were *Yech!* I did not like my looks.

I know, however, that God loves me and wants me to love myself. So I said out loud, "I love you." I spoke this several times. This was very hard, even when I winked. But I was trying a notoriously difficult thing—to change a habit, in this case a habit of self-hatred. So I stuck with it and made some progress, though I was not fully able to change the habit just then. It took several days. But it was worth it!

1.

Low Self-Image

I hate myself," said the woman I was helping as we began to work together with Jesus to deal with a background that included a number of self-image-damaging experiences. She had been conceived out of wedlock to parents who wanted a boy rather than a girl. On top of this, she had been mistreated regularly throughout the 35 years of her life. Assuming, as we all do, that the reason for rejection by the adults in her life was because there was something wrong with her, she turned on herself, adopting toward herself what she believed to be the attitude of her parents and other elders.

I have heard this story hundreds of times over the past three decades since I started working with Jesus in prayer ministry to set captives free (see Luke 4:18–19). Indeed, I have experienced this self-hatred: I was conceived out of wedlock and knew in the womb the rejection of a mother who did not want to be pregnant. I hated the way I looked; I hated my name; I hated life, in spite of the fact that I had it relatively good. I could not imagine that anyone could like me, even after I had come to Christ, or that Jesus would really love me and want me to be a part of His family.

Oh, I kept things pretty well hidden. Most people who hate themselves do. I even achieved quite a bit. I helped others, led the youth group in our church, did well in college athletics, got good grades throughout school, married, became a missionary, got my Ph.D. and have enjoyed a successful career in teaching and writing. But until I was about fifty years old, I hated myself and wished I could be someone else. I was losing a battle with the enemy without even knowing I was a victim in a war between God and Satan.

A word about self-image. The world talks a lot about self-image or self-esteem. It is a major aim of psychological counselors to raise the self-image of anyone who is struggling with feelings of inadequacy, inferiority and negative self-worth. Such counselors spend a lot of time and effort helping their clients to think better of themselves.

Often, though, such efforts are less than maximally successful. There is a reason: *When they evaluate, they start too low.* When, in keeping with the world's understanding of "human beingness," we view humans merely as high-level animals, we can never produce more than a flimsy support for a positive self-image.

If we are to develop a truly solid positive self-image, *we have to start where God starts—with humans in His image.* We are His masterpieces, the highest of God's creations and the one member of His creation that He has redeemed. These facts speak of value. We are highly valued by the Creator and Sustainer of the universe. This is where we can start to deal with self-image. God thinks highly of us. We need to learn to agree with Him.

A Reality beyond Our Reality

I believe that everything we see at our human level has a spiritual dimension that we seldom see. There is a reality beyond the reality we live in. This is what God showed Elijah when he was sulking because Jezebel sought to kill him—there were seven thousand in Israel that Elijah could not see who were still faithful (see 1 Kings 19:18). At another time, when it looked as though there was no way Israel could defeat the Syrians, God showed Israel another reality: "The mountain was full of horses and chariots of fire" (2 Kings 6:17). There was another reality that the Israelites were unaware of.

A very interesting event on this subject occurred when the prophet Balaam was confronted by his donkey, who saw a barrier that the prophet did not see (see Numbers 22:22–34). In this case it was an animal that saw God's reality.

There are many more examples of this throughout the Scriptures. We see them as miracles in human reality. I am seeing them as parts of a separate reality, God's reality.

God is constantly giving those of us who live in human reality glimpses of His reality and inviting us to share it. God's view of us is a part of His reality. And we, lost in our human reality, are often misled into thinking that our reality is the only reality that exists—that our view of ourselves is the correct one when, in fact, God, from His perspective, may see us quite differently.

Before Birth

Ministry experience with hundreds of clients leaves me with the firm impression that major damage to one's self-image often happens before birth. I mentioned the impact that being conceived before my parents married had on me. The scenario seems to be that the first impressions I received while in my mother's womb were feelings of rejection. My mother did not want to be pregnant at age nineteen, with plans for a nursing career that would now have to be interrupted by a hurried wedding. It was a very understandable rejection of a pregnancy, not specifically a rejection of me.

Scientists tell us that somewhere between the fourth and the sixth week of gestation our brains begin recording the events that are taking place and the feelings that accompany those events. At this time, then, I would have become aware that something was going on outside the womb. Whether or not my parents argued about my coming during that time I do not know. It is likely, though, that they did, and that I had awareness that something was wrong. What my brain first recorded, then, was rejection. But as a child in the womb, without the ability to distinguish between rejection of a pregnancy and rejection of me, I felt it was I whom my mother did not want.

Furthermore, in typical childish fashion, I assumed my mother and father knew what they were doing in rejecting me. It would not have occurred to me before birth or for several years after birth that it was my parents who had a problem, not myself. Thus, I assumed that the reason for the rejection I felt must be because there was something wrong with me. So I blamed myself for their problem and adopted toward myself the attitude I felt to be appropriate: self-rejection.

Many of those I have ministered to seem to have developed negative attitudes toward themselves as well as toward others before birth. They sensed that their parents were fighting or that their fathers were violent toward their mothers or that their parents wanted a child of the opposite sex or no child at all. Any of these factors can contribute to a negative self-image and subsequent behavioral issues, all with roots pre-birth.

I once worked with a woman in her mid-thirties who was concerned because she regularly lost control of herself when she disciplined her children. She told me that she over-disciplined them, then felt terribly guilty afterward. In ministry, she reexperienced what seemed like her mother's attempt to abort her in the third month of gestation (later confirmed by her mother). This event was firmly rooted in her memory, and Jesus brought it to the surface. She was then able to forgive her mother, and she never had the problem of over-disciplining her children again.

In addition to such pre-birth life experiences, many individuals have inherited demons whose main assignment is to rob them of positive feelings about themselves. Such spirits might have taken hold of a family through ancestors who were cursed or who cursed themselves, or who took certain vows. Or an ancestor might have belonged to an occult organization such as Freemasonry, Scientology or the Ku Klux Klan and gone through dedications and rituals that gave Satan rights in their families and, therefore, the ability to pass on a sense of rejection to succeeding generations.

Childhood and Youth

Mistreatment in childhood can both produce and reinforce a negative self-image. I worked with a woman whose father and mother beat her regularly, often with no obvious reason. Perhaps the parents felt it was discipline, but she experienced it as abuse, since it was harsh, unloving and frequent. Given such treatment, is it any wonder that she felt worthless and developed strong self-hatred?

Parents are usually the main contributors to low self-image. Often without realizing it, parents take out on their children their own dissatisfaction over the blows that life has dealt them. Even if the child was wanted and there were no significant negative influences before birth, the insecurities and damaging, stuffed memories of parents often result in mistreatment of one kind or another.

An important cause of rejection for some is the death of a parent early in the life of the child. Since young children have no understanding that death is not usually voluntary, they often blame themselves for the fact that the parent never comes back. This happens also in the case of divorce of the parents. *If only I had behaved better,* the child thinks, *my daddy would not have gone away.* When the death is voluntary, the damage may be even greater, since there is often no easily understood reason for the suicide. If adults are unable to explain a suicide, children can develop even more suspicion that they were the cause. "Daddy chose to leave us" is a horrible feeling to have to live with.

Verbal abuse in childhood is a common cause of self-image problems. Parents' or teachers' use of such expressions as *Shame on you* or *You'll never get it right* create great damage in the lives of impressionable children. Though parents seldom intend to do such harm, the child takes the words seriously and, with satanic assistance, turns against himself or herself.

Many of those who come to me for prayer ministry underwent sexual abuse as small children or young adults. The percentage of women in America who have been sexually abused is astounding. And the percentages may be higher in other countries, especially in cultures where disrespect for women is high. Often this abuse is perpetrated by family members—people the victim should be able to trust. This adds feelings of betrayal to the indignity of the misuse of the victim's sexuality.

Sexual abuse is one of Satan's favorite ways of damaging a person's self-image. There is, perhaps, nothing so devastating to a person's dignity than the taking of sexual liberties. Sexual abuse is invasive, both physically and emotionally, leading many to conclude that they have been ruined and, therefore, need not attempt to live up to the moral standards they have been taught.

"I feel like a piece of garbage," they say.

Body image can be an important contributor to self-image problems. During the difficult adolescent years many young people feel uncomfortable with their looks, especially their physiques. Some young people are cruelly ridiculed by their peers for how their looks do not match up with some popular look or image. These cruel comments can have lasting effects on one's self-image and even be painful into adulthood.

Such problems in puberty, which often occur in combination with any number of these other issues, can result in persons cursing themselves or parts of themselves. Frequently, those whose parents wanted a child of the opposite sex curse the sex they have been given. Those who are dissatisfied with their bodies or whose bodies have been misused often speak hateful things to their bodies or to parts of them. A woman in one of my seminars raised her hand and admitted that she has cursed her hair. I suspect that many women (and perhaps some men) have done likewise.

Teachers can contribute to self-image problems. One woman told me how her fifth-grade teacher ridiculed her in front of her classmates regarding a paper she had written. This experience was devastating to her, especially since her work in each grade to that time had been superior and, in addition, her father was the principal of the school. Now, at age 35, she still suffered from the indignity of that rebuke and had a very difficult time forgiving that teacher. She did, however, when she met Jesus in a picturing of that experience. She became gloriously free from a problem that had plagued her for nearly 25 years.

Broken relationships are another source of self-image problems. As children grow into young adulthood, they experience numerous friendships that can get cut off for a variety of reasons. Recently, I ministered to a man whose psyche sustained a considerable amount of damage through a series of rejections by childhood friends.

Others have been hurt by the fact that their parents moved one or more times while they were growing up, forcing them to leave good friends behind and seek to establish new friendships in the new location. Such rending of relationships affects many people deeply, often leading them to conclude that they do not count because their parents did not consult them before making the move. This factor is often more difficult for women since they tend to be more relational than men.

Romantic relationships that get broken can be a major issue in self-image problems. Feelings of rejection or betrayal can easily emerge and lead to emotional crippling, even in the teenage years. Though this source of self-image problems is especially prominent among women, I have ministered to men also who have developed deep feelings of insecurity and failure over broken romances.

Adulthood

Though low self-image usually develops before a person enters adulthood, some adult experiences can produce or reinforce self-rejection or self-hatred. Perhaps the major cause of such problems in adulthood is divorce, usually preceded by a good bit of rejection prior to the actual divorce. A divorced woman typically blames herself for the rejection her husband has expressed toward her. And, if there is betrayal such as an affair, the self-condemnation can be much worse. The feelings of failure accompanying the breakup of a marriage can be devastating.

Even within marriage, the inability of married partners to understand and accept the major sexual differences between men and women can be a primary factor. It seems to me that the primary drive of a woman (in spite of Hollywood) is often a relationship drive rather than a sex drive, whereas for a man the sex drive is prominent. This leads to untold conflict in marriage. With Hollywood projecting male sexuality onto women, the expectations of some men are high that their partners will be as interested as they are in frequent sexual intercourse. When that does not happen, a kind of critical spirit toward one's wife grows. This breeds low self-image.

The breakup of a romantic relationship before marriage can be a major producer or reinforcer of negative self-image. I have ministered to people who were jilted just before the wedding and had never gotten over it.

Business or career failure is another of the producers or reinforcers of negative self-image. In one case, the man I was trying to help had started a series of businesses that became very successful but then crashed. He found it easy to blame himself for every one of the failures, even though they were not all his fault. The enemy was certainly in this, making sure he worked over in his mind every aspect of the failures and took full responsibility for every problem. Not until he experienced Jesus in each of the memories was he able to gain the freedom that allowed him to start again and to succeed. (Please note that we will discuss imaging and memories more fully as we progress though this book.) In this process, though he took full responsibility for the errors that were his, he was able to forgive his business partners who failed or betrayed him as well as forgive himself for the part he played in the failures.

The importance of career for men, and increasingly for women, makes failure or dissatisfaction in the workplace an incredibly sensitive area of life. This fact sets up ready-made self-image destroyers.

Experience the Truth

The enemy of our souls takes advantage of life circumstances and cultural standards to put us down. From these experiences, he crafts lies and teaches us to believe them. He often invades our self-talk, getting us to do his work of repeating his lies. Satan will do everything possible to keep us from discovering our true identity. In this way, he gains many captives.

How do we dig out of the holes created by such experiences—and loose ourselves from Satan's grip? In John 8:32 we read in most translations: "You will know the truth, and the truth will set you free." Too often, believing another of the enemy's lies, we assume that the "truth" John had in mind was cognitive knowledge. Not so. The Greek understanding of the knowledge that can set us free is that it is *experiential knowledge*, the kind of knowledge that comes through experience, not simply from knowing facts. This is knowledge that is tested by experience and applied to life situations. Furthermore, the word used there for *knowledge* implies that when that knowledge is experienced, it will be obeyed.

So, knowledge that is experienced and obeyed, under God's direction, sets us free. Actually, it is God Himself who sets us free, but He uses certain knowledge experienced and obeyed to do the job.

Do you know who you are?

EXERCISE

Let's begin to explore the process of "faith picturing." God has put into His creation the ability to imagine. In brief, God has given us the ability to comprehend truth through pictures. We can use this to help us feel closer to Jesus.

Though some of us are better at this than others, the effort to picture truths about God is worth it. You might, for instance, picture in your mind Jesus healing the man who is being lowered down through the roof by his friends (see Mark 2:1–12) or see Him talking to Zacchaeus who is up in a tree (see Luke 19:1–10).

For this exercise, read these words from Mark 10:13–16:

Then they brought little children to Him, that He might touch them; but the disciples rebuked those who brought them. But when Jesus saw it, He was greatly displeased and said to them, "Let the little children come to Me, and do not forbid them; for of such is the kingdom of God. Assuredly, I say to you, whoever does not receive the kingdom of God as a little child will by no means enter it." And He took them up in His arms, laid His hands on them, and blessed them.

Now close your eyes and picture Jesus calling the little children to Himself. As you picture this story, imagine His love for the children and the tenderness with which He welcomes them and blesses them.

Now see if you can imagine yourself in the group as one of those little ones. Can you see how He might put His arm gently around you? If this is difficult for you, simply continue to picture the Bible story in your mind.

2

Satan Is Not Happy about Us

Most Christians believe that before God created human beings, Lucifer/Satan was in second place in the universe. He served God and was one of the highest archangels, if not the highest. Then he rebelled. In the Isaiah passage considered to be about Lucifer's fall we read:

> Bright morning star, you have fallen from heaven! . . . You were determined to climb up to heaven and to place your throne above the highest stars. . . . You said you would climb to the tops of the clouds and be like the Almighty. But instead, you have been brought down to the deepest part of the world of the dead.
>
> Isaiah 14:12–15 GNT

Though it is a mystery why Satan rebelled, my theory is that it had something to do with God's creation of humans. If Lucifer was in second place in creation, he would be dropped to third place as soon as God created a human in His own image—for no angel is in God's image, not even the highest angel, Lucifer. Only humans have been created in God's image, a little lower than God Himself (Psalm 8:5, correctly translated). And this fact could have made Lucifer jealous and bent on revenge. Such a scenario would explain why Satan hates God and the masterpiece of His creation, humans.

Throughout Scripture we see Satan warring against God. We see him attacking Adam and Eve in the Garden, deceiving them into relinquishing their authority over the creation (see Luke 4:6). This warring came to its culmination at Calvary, where Satan lost the war for time and eternity. For some reason, though, God has allowed him to continue to be active in the human context, working his schemes to try to destroy us. Failing in his quest to dislodge God, he turns to attacking God's masterpiece. Thus, we live our lives in a war zone, behind enemy lines.

We are, then, whether we like it or not, major participants in God's war with Satan. God created us and gave us authority over the universe (see Psalm 8:6–8). Perhaps the universe had been under Lucifer's authority before he fell. In any event, once God put a human in the world, Satan's plan was to regain the authority and control he once had by stealing it from God. If he could just deceive the man into obeying him, he could have his former territory back. So, he tempted Adam and Eve, and they, through disobeying God, gave their authority to Satan. That is why Satan could say to Jesus: "The kingdoms of this world with all of their power and wealth have all been handed over to me, and I can give them to anyone I choose" (see Luke 4:6).

Since it was a man who gave the world to Satan, God's plan was to win it back through a Man, Christ Jesus, the "last Adam," the "second man" (see 1 Corinthians 15:21–22, 45, 47). This He did and the war is won, but it continues. We call the continuation of this war "spiritual warfare."

Satan's Primary Attacks

From my own story and that of many others, I have come to the conclusion that the main place where spiritual warfare occurs is inside, not outside of us. Though it is true that Satan attacks churches, families and nations, his major aim is to destroy *people*. And he does this by turning us against ourselves. Demons even seem to train us to repeat to ourselves the self-condemnation and rejection they want us to feel.

Demons can invade our self-talk, getting us to voice our displeasure over who we are. These words and attitudes give Satan rights in our lives and power over us. Many people curse themselves by saying things like, "I hate my body" (or some part of it), "I am so stupid," "I wish [some part of me] were bigger/smaller," "I wish I had never been born."

Our enemy uses a variety of life circumstances to turn us against ourselves. Being conceived out of wedlock is one of them. People who have suffered sexual or physical abuse often come to regard themselves as refuse. As one young lady who had been raped said to me, "I felt I had been ruined, so why should I try to live right?"

Verbal abuse can also result in self-hatred. Many have told me that their self-image took a beating whenever they heard their parents say things like, "You're not very bright" or "Why can't you do what I tell you?" or "You'll never amount to anything" or "Leave me alone; I'm busy."

Our enemy, Satan, specializes in deceiving us. Sometimes he lies. More often he uses deceit to mislead us into lying to ourselves. "Your grades are not as good as your brother's," many parents say. And that may be true. The parents did not lie. But the upshot of the impression it makes is more negative than the parents intended. This kind of statement is greatly used by Satan to damage a person's self-esteem: It leads the child to believe that since he is not as good as his brother in grades, he is not good at anything and is inferior in everything to everyone, not just the brother.

Likewise with a comment like, "You ought to be ashamed of yourself." This comment is often made in reaction to something a person has done. But it is a comment on the person's *being* not her *doing*. Ashamed of your*self*, not of the thing you have *done*. And, again, the enemy is right there to deceive her into turning against herself.

Our enemy uses lots of words and actions to turn us against ourselves. There are words like these that shame us. There are abusive actions that intimidate us. There are mistakes we make that we regret to the extent that we condemn or even curse ourselves.

The standards of society can also afford the enemy opportunities to get us to put ourselves down. In American society, for example, the standards for a woman's body are impossible for most women to attain. But many try through dieting, or even extreme measures such as surgery or anorexia, to achieve that ideal body size and shape. For guys, achieving in sports may be the goal. And if we get chosen last or fail to make the team or never do as well as we, the coach or the fans expect, we feel miserable. For some who never achieve in their careers or own a prestigious car or home, life can seem not worth living.

One way or another, Satan likes to bring things across our paths that we interpret as meaning we are not worth very much. Though we may hear preaching or read the Bible or books on self-image that tell us we are valuable in God's sight, our feelings never let us believe what we hear or read. And feelings are more where we live than thoughts and facts.

The result is that many of us live with a very low self-image.

Three Enemies

Generally, we have three enemies that block us from developing a healthy self-image: emotional problems, demons and bad habits.

First, the way we handle our emotions determines whether or not they become problems, basic things that tear us down. Something happens that gets us angry, and we cannot shake the anger. Or something scares us, and we develop a fear problem. Or we do something wrong and our mothers shout, "What's the matter with you?" And all of a sudden a load of guilt and shame crashes into our consciousness. People might have hurt us badly, even to the point of abuse, and we just cannot forgive them, even though we know that Jesus requires us to forgive. We cannot get rid of the emotional baggage, even though we know that Jesus can free people from such things.

In short, *we are saved but not free*. Where is the freedom we were promised when we came to Christ?

The second basic enemy we face is demons. Though many people fear demons, thinking they are strong and will cause a fight, they really are not strong. They are a secondary issue—secondary to emotional and spiritual issues—and get their power from humans. People who persist in emotional problems give demons the legal right to live inside.

Consider, for instance, these emotional and spiritual issues:

Anger. Uncontrolled anger puts one in danger of infestation by demons. This is a rule of the universe.

Shame and guilt. Everyone who has given his or her life to Jesus needs to give Him all shame and guilt or risk becoming demonized. Those who hold fast to shame or guilt are "sitting ducks" for demons to infest.

Fear and worry. These issues also open the doors wide for demons to enter. For many individuals, these are embedded habits that function as part of their personalities.

Rejection. Another big one. Rejection, for many, starts in the womb with an unwanted pregnancy. This opens a person to rejection of many kinds during childhood and adulthood.

These and many similar characteristics invite demons in. From that vantage point, they can affect our self-image, keeping us from knowing and acting as the people we are intended to be.

Demons, then, live in those who are governed by fear or shame or other such emotions and those who cannot or will not forgive. Dealing with problem number one, the emotional and spiritual issues, weakens the hold demons have and makes it easier to get them out without a fight.

We can compare this to rats and garbage. If you see rats, you know some garbage is attracting them. In our lives, it is possible to have both emotional garbage (such as unforgiveness) and spiritual garbage (such as curses or being dedicated to Satan). This garbage attracts and feeds demons, and gives them their strength. If you deal with the garbage, then the sustenance of the rats is removed, and they can be gotten rid of without much difficulty.

The third of three enemies to a good self-image may be a bit more complicated. It involves dealing with *bad habits*. It is often the case that bad habits are underlying the emotional and spiritual issues we need to overcome. If anger is the issue, for instance, we first need immediate freedom from the emotional problem of rash anger and then dislodging of the demons. Next comes the ability to stay free from the old patterns. This will mean constant vigilance and strong determination not to fall back into the old ways. We badly need the presence and power of Jesus to help us keep challenging the old habits and develop new habits—freedom habits.[1]

EXERCISE

Are you aware of being affected by the three "enemies" discussed in this chapter: emotional problems, demons and bad habits?

Think of any ways that Satan uses these enemies in your life. Think in particular if there is someone who hurt you regarding one of these areas and whom you need to forgive.

Now think about that individual or event with Jesus in the picture. Knowing that you are forgiven, can you choose to forgive? When there are those I need to forgive, I like to picture them in my hands as I give them to Jesus. If there is to be revenge, let Jesus do it.

3

Inner or Deep-Level Healing

M any Christians have been gloriously saved but are not free. They are redeemed but the old habits hang on. They look in the mirror and see the same old person. Oh, they experienced an exhilarating feeling when they first gave themselves to Christ, but the noticeable change did not last—maybe a couple of weeks or a couple of months, and then life was just about the same as it used to be.

Some gave wonderful testimonies of the changes they had experienced after their salvation. But they may have been faking their walk in the new life, afraid to admit that their experience was not what was promised and concluding that something must be wrong with them.

And they heard the inside voice taunting them with words such as, *See, I told you it wouldn't work.* And things went back to "normal," a terribly disappointing normal that invited the old self-image to take its familiar place. Satan uses these reactions to tear down even persons who are pretty solid emotionally. It is not unusual for individuals who have impressive achievements to fight low self-image and feel they are losing the battle. Life is hard for most (perhaps all) people, and the reactions to it are often emotionally crippling.

But there is hope. God enables us to work with Jesus to bring freedom from toxic responses to life events and the demons that attach themselves to attitudes and habits. And it is available to those who either have not discovered who they are or have forgotten. This approach deals with the wounding by looking *with Jesus* at the painful events that caused it.

Jesus is omnipresent. He was there when the event(s) happened. He is, further, omnipotent. He can heal and set captives free. And, as we will learn later in this book, He works in partnership with us to carry out His will.

The approach is called "inner healing," what I like to call "deep-level healing." It is simply a matter of going back in our memories and picturing a hurtful or scary event, while at the same time asking Jesus to help us experience His presence there. With our eyes on Jesus, we can more easily give Him the pain and forgive as we have been forgiven.

Some people are afraid to trust such picturing in this manner, feeling that it might be misleading or even New Age. They point out the potential for false memories and the danger in trusting them. Though that is a risk, I believe the ability to picture is God-given and meant for our good.

Indeed, memory specialists point out that we think in pictures. Both dreams and prophecies are varieties of picturing that God uses. As for the New Agers' use of picturing, they indeed make use of the technique, recognizing that it is powerful and can be used under satanic power. But nearly every technique that God or humans have brought into existence can be used either by God or by Satan. The techniques are neutral and can be harnessed either for evil or for good. They are not evil or good in essence but only in use.

I have found for countless people that inner healing under the guidance of the Holy Spirit can help bring about freedom, healing and change of self-image.

The Plan in Action

To help you understand this concept further, I present a typical story of a woman who came to me for ministry. I will call her Jill. As she was able to experience deep healing, she also experienced changes in her self-image.

Jill grew up in a Christian home, loved by family and friends but hating herself. She did well in school but, when complimented on her work, did not allow her academic abilities to affect her self-image.

Jill was outgoing and had many friends. She went to church and Bible study groups regularly and did not hesitate to speak up about her faith. She married and had two children.

This was her public life. Her private life was another matter. She went to various Christian counselors, hoping to get a grip on her inner stuff. She confessed to her counselors that she felt unaccepted by her friends and work associates, fearful for her job, inadequate as a wife and mother and angry with herself for mistakes she made, to the point of planning suicide.

She hated herself and certain people who had mistreated her. She was not free to claim freedom from these internal enemies.

Jill felt lonely and dissatisfied with marriage and parenting. Her children bugged her, and the frequent arguments she had with her husband wore her down. She carried out her wifely and motherly duties acceptably but with little satisfaction and the constant fear that her insecurities were rubbing off on the kids.

Many of Jill's activities and choices increased her shame and guilt. She prayed a lot, but God seemed far away and not interested in her problems. A male co-worker took a liking to her, and she fantasized about what life would be like with him, which increased her shame. She wondered if the smiling faces of her church friends hid problems such as hers.

In short, Jill was quite "normal." Her struggles were similar to those of many of the young women she worshiped with every Sunday. But neither church nor professional counseling had helped. She was not free.

When she came to me, I spent about half an hour getting acquainted with her. I prayed that God would meet her and grant her the freedom that she was promised when she gave her life to Jesus.

I explained to her that Satan hates our freedom and seeks to take it away. Then I followed a simple plan to deal with the memories that held her captive. Knowing that our memories start about four weeks after conception, I asked her to picture Jesus with His hands stretched out toward her, with a sperm in one hand and an egg in the other. I then asked Jill what she wanted Jesus to do with that sperm and egg.

"Given that He has thrown away trillions of sperms and eggs," I said, "should He just throw these away and not make you? Or should He put them together and make you?"

This was not an easy choice for Jill. Her feelings told her she did not want to be conceived. But she knew the answer Jesus wanted, and that giving a different answer would keep her in the captivity she was trying to overcome. She reasoned this out and eventually allowed herself to give Jesus' answer. She was able to picture Jesus' putting His hands together to make her.

At that point I blessed each month of gestation, canceling any spiritual stuff such as dedications and curses that were uttered, including any curses of not being wanted. I mentioned that not being wanted had been a big problem for me, and that I, too, had felt this rejection in the womb.

Next, I invited Jill to picture Jesus with her in each month of gestation, giving each month to Him, leading to birth, which I asked her to picture with Jesus in it and holding her and blessing her as a newborn baby.

From that point we went from year to year looking for important events in Jill's memory. Jill pictured Jesus in each event and gave each event to Him. The point was to help her experience the truth that Jesus was there and handling whatever the event required to get it healed. Whether sin, curses, unforgiveness, fear, rejection or shame, she talked about each emotion with Jesus and gave each one to Him.

In short, Jill replayed her whole life with a new experience of Jesus' presence in each event. She received emotional and spiritual release from the captivity in which she had been bound. We spent most of our time getting these emotional roots healed. When unforgiveness was uncovered, she forgave.

Then it was time to see if there were any enemy spirits attached to Jill's emotional and spiritual wounds.

Demons attach themselves to such wounds, working in secret to mess up the lives of victims. We can expect demons to attach to emotional issues such as those listed above. We can also expect demons to attach to spiritual issues such as curses, dedications, vows, inherited family spirits, occult spirits and the like. We can claim the power of Jesus to cancel all enemy rights given through these emotional and spiritual avenues.

In Jill's case, family spirits were inherited from a grandmother who was a witch. With that information in hand, I knew it was also likely that Jill had been dedicated to Satan and was the recipient of satanic "blessings." So I first claimed Jesus' power to break the grip of inherited spirits and all other witchcraft spirits.

I then commanded the demon of witchcraft to come to attention and asked what legal right he had to be there. He spoke through Jill to answer my question, saying, "I have no rights now." I then covered him (verbally) with the blood of Jesus and commanded him to gather all his helpers and to be locked in a box.

I did a similar thing with each of the demons attached to the emotions that she had identified when she told her life story. There were spirits of fear and worry, shame and guilt, anger, rejection, self-hatred and several others.

We focused especially on forgiveness, since she told me she had a very hard time forgiving people. I again asked her to picture herself in the hurtful events with Jesus there and to give her hurts to Him, also turning over the individuals to Jesus. This exercise helped free her from the anger and unforgiveness that had dogged her steps and taken her joy. We also gave a lot of attention to her self-hatred and the difficulty of forgiving herself as Jesus had forgiven her.

When she had given all her hurts to Jesus, thus taking away the demons' legal rights and breaking their power, I asked the angels to gather the boxes full of demons and take them to Jesus. Then I asked Jesus to send the demons away, and I forbade any to come back or to send others to torment Jill.

At the end of this prayer time, I noted the change on Jill's face as she entered for the first time into the freedom she had been promised. She felt changed from the inside out.

A Changed Perception

Jill's perception of who she is changed dramatically during that session. She had come to Christ and to all intents and purposes was a "good Christian." She was genuinely committed to Jesus and tried to show that in her behavior.

But, as I have mentioned, she was not free. She lived in disappointment, feeling that there must be more to Christianity than she was experiencing. She was unaware of the enemy's influence on her self-image. She had no understanding of how he saw to it that she kept her eyes on the bad stuff in her life. She lived as if she were driving with her eyes fixed on the rearview mirror.

Jill did not recognize that our enemy was working constantly to put her down. He used a number of devices that he employs against women, such as mistreatment by men, dissatisfaction with her body and insecurity in relationships. Satan hoped that she would internalize the negative influences that touched her at an early age and keep the resulting negative self-perceptions always with her.

When Jill considered the Scriptures that show how highly Jesus regards women, she gained a new perspective. Then, by working with Holy Spirit–guided picturing, she was able to give the negative things to Jesus and lift her head in victory over the enemy.

Jill—like most of us—needed to square her feelings with the truth about Jesus' attitude toward her. She sort of knew how important she was to Him but did not feel it. And since we live largely in our feelings, this was a very important issue.

The next step in this process of deep-level healing is the development of what I call a "freedom habit." Having taken these steps toward a new self-perception, Jill needed to work on replacing her old habits.

I suggested that Jill use a mirror to talk to herself about what she had experienced. She could speak to herself various words of self-love and self-acceptance to help her maintain her freedom. The important thing was to love herself and accept herself as Jesus loves and accepts her. I recommended that Jill see herself in the mirror with a crown on her head. She is a princess in Jesus' Kingdom. That is who she is.

Throughout this journey, you, too, can gain a new perspective about yourself. But remember: You need to practice embracing it. In the following pages I will help you bolster a new perception and add to it.

Do you know and experience who you are?

EXERCISE

As you continue your work to face the three "enemies" of emotional problems, demons and bad habits, be aware of any memories that come to mind. Give each episode to Jesus, feeling His acceptance of you and letting Him help you forgive those who have hurt you.

For this exercise, ask Jesus to help you forgive yourself for any way that self-rejection has contributed to a negative self-image.

4

In the Image of God

So I'm in God's image, am I? If that is true, why don't
I feel like it? Why do I feel like a pile of manure?" I
cannot count the number of times I have heard something
like this from those with poor self-image.

We live in our feelings. Even if you are left-brained and
cognitive in the extreme, you live in your feelings. Communication specialists tell us that the meanings of the
speech events in which we participate are primarily felt
and only secondarily reasoned. Though we may later re-
vise our interpretations of an event, our first attempt at
interpretation is a feeling attempt, not a thinking one.

Types of Memory

An interesting analysis of memory was published by Daniel
Schacter while he was chair of Harvard's psychology department. In *Searching for Memory*, he describes three types
of memory systems: procedural, semantic and episodic.

In *procedural* memory are stored all of the directions that enable us to move, type, drive our cars and, in short, perform the activities of life. Though this is an important part of our memory system, we will not further treat it here.

The second type of memory is what Schacter calls *semantic*. This is where we store perceptions of logic, reasoning, linear thinking, information, facts and the like. This is the part of memory that our schooling is largely involved in developing. Unfortunately, a good bit of what goes on in church is aimed at this part of our memory as well. I say unfortunately, because this is not the part of our memory in which we "live and move and have our being."

The memory place in which we live is called *episodic*. This is picture memory. It is here that we store life experiences in images, including our feelings about the experience, our reactions, our intuitions. It is because this is where we live that pictures are usually more powerful than words, unless the words constitute stories or what has been called "word pictures." The things stored in this part of our memory are usually influential in our lives and more easily retrievable than the things stored in semantic memory.

The influence of picture memory can be seen when we consider what we remember most easily from lectures and sermons. Even for intellectuals who have carefully honed their semantic memories, it is the illustrations, the images, the pictures, the stories more than the logical propositions that are most readily recalled. I believe this is why Jesus regularly presented His teachings in the word pictures that we call parables. He spoke of Himself as the Water of Life, the Bread of Life, the Good Shepherd. He pictured God as the Father and Himself as the Son. He drew for us pictures of a good Samaritan, a prodigal son, a conversation between a rich man in hell and Lazarus in paradise, an unjust steward, a lost coin, a lost sheep and on and on. He hardly taught anything without presenting it in picture form. By communicating in this way, He appealed to this important part of memory and to the feelings that lodge there.

So, if we want to combat the emotional devastation of low self-image, we need to do and say things that will appeal to this part of our memories. We need to store the understanding of a healthy self-image in picture memories, not simply word (semantic) memories. We want to *feel* the truth, not simply to know it in a cognitive way. We understand and describe our position in words, true, but it must not end there. It must be attached to our feelings.

I believe God wants you to *feel* who you are. He wants you to hold your chin high, not in arrogance but in self-assurance. He wants you to live in recognition of the fact that you are God's masterpiece and "God don't make junk."

The Image of God

To live the kind of Christian life we desire to live, we need fortification against the lies of the enemy. Much of his battle against us is centered in his ability to deceive us. Though Satan is the father of lies (see John 8:44), he does not always lie. He is too clever for that.

Deceit is much more dangerous than lies. Lies are often so obvious that the enemy's chances of getting us to believe them are not very good. But deceit uses truth to mislead us. "I am such a sinner—how could God love me?" is the kind of question that often comes to those of us with low self-esteem. It is a deceiving question because the first part is not wholly untrue and, given the first part, the last part seems logical.

The enemy would not likely say something like this: "You're not made in the image of God." That would be too blatant, too obvious a lie. But he would play off the truth of our failures to lead us logically to a conclusion that denies our position of second place in the universe.

I grew up in a church that focused on human failure to the extent that we thought we were being humble when we spoke or thought negatively about ourselves. God's love was not cast as something positive rooted in the fact of our creation. His love, rather, was framed by our "no-good-ness" with the perspective that God accepts "dirty, rotten sinners" into His family. With this image fixed firmly in our psyches, we spent a lot of time confessing our sins and not much time exhibiting and glorying in our position as Godlike beings.

This attitude is prevalent in our hymns and liturgies. We are constantly (in many churches every week) confessing that "we have done things that we should not have done and left undone things that we should have done," as if beating ourselves up is an important spiritual discipline. Not that there is no truth regarding our sinful behavior. But harping on that fact, regularly picturing ourselves as sinners, keeps us emotionally low, thus giving the enemy victory over us.

I like the story of the believer who had done something for which he was deeply sorry and came to God fully repentant: "O God, I have committed this sin and beg Your forgiveness."

God's response was, "What sin?"

The man had confessed his sin; it was immediately forgiven and forgotten by God. Between him and God, it was just as if he had never sinned.

God worked from the fact of the relationship, not from the gravity of the sin. The man did the right thing by acknowledging his failure. But he would be doing the wrong thing to be begging God's pardon continually for something already forgiven and forgotten.

Our position as God's image bearers, plus the redemptive activity of Jesus, takes care of the guilt so that when the enemy comes to prod us with our failure, we can simply remind him that the matter has been taken care of. The picture of us as "dirty rotten sinners" has been replaced by a picture of us free and clean.

At Creation God said that humans "will be like us and resemble us" (Genesis 1:26 GNT).

> So God created human beings, making them to be like himself. He created them male and female, blessed them, and said, "Have many children, so that your descendants will live all over the earth and bring it under their control." . . . God looked at everything he had made, and he was very pleased.
>
> Genesis 1:27–28, 31 GNT

Now God says to you, "I have created you in My own image, after My own likeness."

There is only one being that God makes such a statement to. He never says that to any angel or any animal; only humans bear His image. This is an incredible distinction between us and the rest of creation. And, as I suggested in chapter 1, Satan is jealous of us. He, though a prestigious and powerful angel, is not nor ever can be in God's image.

What Does This Mean?

What exactly does it mean to be made in the image of God? No one really knows! Commentaries on these verses suggest that our creativity is an important part of the image of God in us. Some suggest that our ability to think, feel and reason is a key ingredient of that image. Without doubt our emotions are an important part. Our ability to choose is a part of our Godlikeness. But since we know that Satan and his angels once chose to rebel against God, we cannot point to ourselves as the only beings with the ability to choose. Those angels apparently could choose to challenge God's right to run the universe.

Psalm 8 helps us a bit, even though, as we will see in a moment, many of our translations are not theologically accurate in the way they render the word *elohim* in verse 5. In this psalm David is extolling God's greatness as demonstrated in creation: "O LORD, our Lord, your greatness is seen in all the world!" he says in verse 1 (GNT). He refers, then, to the praise offered even by children and babies, followed by a statement concerning God's security and power to defeat His enemies.

Then he looks up to the heavens, saying, "When I look at the sky, which you have made, at the moon and the stars, which you set in their places—what are human beings, that you think of them; mere mortals, that you care for them?" (Psalm 8:3–4 GNT).

David looks at the enormous heavenly panorama, as he must have night after night as a boy while tending his father's sheep. If you have ever pondered the night sky, you know how easy it is to feel insignificant.

"How could You care about a being that is so small in comparison to the galaxies You have set in their places?" David asks.

The answer comes in a way that changes our perspective radically. We are small, yes, when compared to the heavens. But insignificant? No, not at all. So David shakes himself out of any discouragement that might accompany his view of our smallness as compared to the vastness of the heavens and says, "Yet you made them [humans] inferior only to yourself; you crowned them with glory and honor. You appointed them rulers over everything you made; you placed them over all creation" (Psalm 8:5–6 GNT).

Literally the verse says, "inferior only to *elohim*." A little lower than God Himself! And, in addition, crowned with glory and honor, created to rule over all creation.

I think it is of interest that many of our Bible versions mistranslate *elohim* in this verse as "angels." "Angels" is a possible translation linguistically, but it is not possible theologically, since we are not at all inferior to the angels. (We discuss this more thoroughly in the next chapter.) The mistake was made by early translators of the Old Testament into Greek (called the Septuagint). My guess is that *they were struggling with self-image* and could not bring themselves to claim what God wants us to claim—a place immediately under Himself.

Since the early Church used the Septuagint, the author of Hebrews quotes this verse using the word *angels* (see Hebrews 2:7, 9). But he uses the term with reference to a time, not to a physical or spiritual position. That is, when the author of Hebrews says that Jesus was made "for a little while lower than the angels" so that He could bring about our redemption, he is referring to the time of Jesus' descent to earth, not to His position in creation. It is, I believe, the position of human beings in creation that is in view in the original of Psalm 8:5.

We are created in God's image, a little lower than God Himself in the universe, *but like God Himself.* What are we going to do with this truth, especially if we do not feel as though we hold this high position?

Personally, for many years I challenged the truth of these statements in my mind. I wondered how God could think of me so highly while I felt so unworthy. It was not until I dealt with the fact that I had been rejected in the womb, until I *forgave* my parents and *accepted* myself as valid in God's sight, that I stopped challenging His judgment concerning me.

I discovered who I am.

What Do We Do with This Position?

Imagine a person who is given a gift of, say, five billion dollars with instructions that the money be used to help and encourage people the giver loves. Instead of using it wisely, however, the person buries it and never uses the money except for giving token amounts here and there.

Add to this picture an enemy who takes advantage of those who are dear to the giver and who should receive the help. The enemy, observing that the receiver of the money does not use it nor plans to use it according to the giver's instructions, carries on the attacks with little hindrance.

We would say that person is not being responsible. He is expected to use that money to fulfill the purposes the giver had in mind. He fails to do what is expected of him, giving the enemy space to do whatever he wants.

Being in the image of God, we have infinitely more power than our enemy has. The enemy cannot outpower us. But he can bluff us very effectively. And he does.

Being in the image of God has implications for the use of this power in spiritual warfare. Jesus, our model as to how we should wield it, spent His life using that power to show His love. His was a message of love and power. We, His followers, though we often do a good job on the love part, seem to have forgotten the power part. But that is an important aspect of our heritage.

Jesus said, "When you see demons being cast out, you know the Kingdom is near" (see Matthew 12:28; Luke 11:20). That being true, what do we say if we claim to be following Jesus but never deal with demons? If the Church is not casting out demons, what does this show us about our relationship to the One we claim to be following? Are we ignoring an important part of God's image?

Our rightful position is with Jesus, drinking in His love, but also warring to defeat His enemy. We are expected to partner with Jesus in love and power. We are to treat all of God's masterpieces as God intended, fulfilling God's intent by recognizing truly who we are and acting out our love and our power by freeing those who are held captive by the enemy.

Being in the image of God is an incredible honor, but there are implications. Perhaps the major implication is that God's cause becomes our cause as we partner with Him in extending His Kingdom—the Kingdom of love and power.

EXERCISE

Review the mirror exercise found in the Introduction to this book. Practice your own self-acceptance using the mirror. Then picture yourself as a young child walking with Jesus in a garden, holding His hand.

5

Compared to Angels

Angels play an important role in the workings of God in human life. From Genesis to Revelation we read how they are involved in a variety of activities serving God. Following is a sampling of Bible references to their activities. Angels:

- Guarded the way to the Tree of Life (see Genesis 3:24)
- Gave the Law (see Galatians 3:19; Hebrews 2:2)
- Announced the birth of Samson (see Judges 13:3–5), of John (see Luke 1:7–20) and of Jesus (see Luke 1:26–38)
- Warned Joseph to take Mary and the Child to Egypt (see Matthew 2:13)
- Ministered to Jesus after the temptations (see Matthew 4:11)
- Ministered to Jesus during His Passion (see Luke 22:43)
- Were present at the tomb of Jesus (see Matthew 28:2–7)

- Rolled back the stone after the crucifixion (see Matthew 28:2)
- Announced Jesus' resurrection at the tomb (see Matthew 28:1–7)
- Were present at the ascension (see Acts 1:10–11)
- Will be with Jesus at His Second Coming (see Matthew 25:31)
- Will be at the Judgment (see Matthew 13:39–49)
- Are media of revelation (see Daniel 9:21–27; 10:10–21)
- Rescue God's people (see Numbers 20:16)

These and many other scriptural references show that angels are indeed important players in God's drama. In every major event and most minor events they are there, doing God's bidding, operating in God's power, serving God's purposes.

Angels are truly impressive, tempting us to assume that they must be God's choicest creation, but they are not—for not one of them is in God's image.

Where, then, do angels fit? The author of the book of Hebrews attempts to answer that question: "Angels are only servants [slaves]—spirits sent [from God] to care for people who will inherit salvation" (Hebrews 1:14 NLT).

They are "only" servants/slaves, sent to care for us. So who is more important: the caregiver or the one being cared for? We know the answer. If the angels are impressive, then we who are above them are more impressive.

Their impressiveness leads many to assume that they are a higher order of being than humans. But in spite of what many people think, it is we, not angels, who are the higher order. In spite of the fact that our physical bodies limit us in many ways, so that we seem frail in comparison to angels, it is *we*, not *they*, who have been created just a little lower than God Himself (see Psalm 8:5). And they exist to serve God and us.

Yes, angels are impressive, but no angel is in God's image. Angels envy us and are curious about what God is going to do with us. They want to "look into" what God is doing (1 Peter 1:12).

Indeed, our status vis-à-vis angels is made clear in 1 Corinthians 6:3: "Do you not know that we shall judge angels?" We humans will judge the angels, signaling once again that we are higher than these spirits that God sends to serve us. That is who we are.

The Parts of Humanity

Let me mention a word here about the human makeup. There have been endless discussions concerning the design of human beings. Some say we are but a single entity. Some say we have a material part, our bodies, and an immaterial part, our souls. Others contend that there are three parts: body, soul and spirit. The soul, in this definition, is made up of mind, emotions and will.

Personally, I see no need for the word *soul*. My preference is to speak of five parts: *spirit*, *body*, *mind*, *emotions* and *will*. Whatever one's preference might be, it is important to recognize the presence of the human spirit—that part of us that can connect with God. Psychologists tend to recognize only the soul in that they recognize mind, emotions and will, making no distinction between soul and spirit. And, we must admit, making a distinction between soul and spirit is a difficult thing.

I (along with many others) will postulate, though, that there is a part of us that I will call *spirit* that is the central immaterial part of us. This is the part that connects with God when we come to Christ and, I believe, connects with members of our families and others with whom we have a close, bonding relationship. My guess is that this spirit part of us is that which is made in the image of God. Someone has said, "We *are* a spirit; we *live in* a body." That statement makes sense to me.

In ministry, I find that problems we might identify as spirit problems and those we might identify as emotional problems are hard to distinguish from each other. Is anger, for example, an emotional or a spiritual problem? It seems to be both. Likewise with fear or shame or a host of other problems that manifest themselves through the emotions, making it likely that spirit problems are regularly, if not always, expressed as emotional problems.

I believe it is our spirit, the central part of us, that comes to Christ when we accept Him for salvation. When we respond, this is where the Holy Spirit comes to dwell.

Evil Angels

Apparently when Satan rebelled a fair number of angels took his side. These are the beings we call demons. Their job is to implement Satan's schemes. High on the list of demonic activities, then, is keeping us ignorant of our God-given status, our true identity.

Satan's demons work hard on us. They push us to compare ourselves to others and to find ourselves wanting. They goad us to anger and hatred toward others. They specialize in getting us to feel shame and guilt. Fear is another of their specialties. They take ordinary feelings, exaggerate any problems that might result from those feelings and help their victims develop hurtful habits out of their overreactions.

Demons like to build on inherited flaws such as family curses or evil dedications. People often inherit demons without knowing it or believing it. It is demonic angels that are in charge of implementing the satanic presence that comes our way. In addition, the satanic angels deaden the influence of God's activities in churches and other places where God is honored.

In short, demons do Satan's dirty work and turn people against themselves and others. They also carry on a war in the heavenlies.

Ministering Spirits

Perhaps the major function of the angels who serve God is to "minister" to us. We do not know much specifically about their functions, but apparently we are important enough to have angels assigned to help to us. Two translations of Hebrews 1:14 (NKJV and GNT) word it this way:

Are they [angels] not all ministering spirits sent forth to minister for those who will inherit salvation?

What are the angels, then? They are spirits who serve God and are sent by him to help those who are to receive salvation.

This passage assumes that God's people are so valuable that He assigns angels to assist us. Whatever we need to have or do, it is the job of the angels to help make it happen. Do we know how important we are as participants in God's Kingdom?

EXERCISE

A friend of mine once asked a demon if there were angels in the room where he was ministering. The demon replied, "Yes, lots of them."

My friend correctly concluded that they were there to assist him as he ministered. He could not see them, but the truth is that they were there just as the army of God was there for Elisha in the scriptural event recorded in 2 Kings 6:17.

Do your best to picture the truth of the army of angels surrounding you as you live your life.

6

Chosen before Creation

She was the fourth girl in a Chinese family. I will call her Ruby. Now 39 years old, Ruby had just been told that her body was full of cancer.

"Have you ever tried to be a boy?" I asked.

"Every second of my life," she replied.

"Have you ever cursed your body?" was my next question.

"Yes, thousands of times."

She then told me how as an early teen she had tied a cloth tightly across her chest to conceal the development of her breasts. She had for all of her life been consumed with shame over being female and thus a big disappointment to her parents. Ruby lived under a double curse: the curse of "unwantedness" coming from her parents and extended family, plus the lifetime of curses she had put on herself. And her unwanted, cursed body was responding by developing cancer.

Ruby's story is a bit more dramatic than most. And, incidentally, God healed her. But many of us either know or suspect that our parents did not want us. Either they did not want to be pregnant at all (as in my parents' case), or they wanted a child of the opposite sex (as with Ruby). The reaction, then, can vary from self-rejection, self-hatred or self-loathing to attempts at suicide, some of which are successful.

God got what He wanted, a child of the sex He had preordained. But Ruby's unconscious memories were very much alive and affected her consciousness.

A man I will call John came with an intensely guilty conscience over his very existence and especially over being male. At age 35 he could not shake the feeling that he did not deserve to exist. As we looked for clues in his roots, he told me that his mother had given birth to a boy, then a girl who died soon after birth, and then him. He felt keenly that he was merely a substitute for the sister who had died, but an inadequate substitute, since he was male and his parents wanted a replacement for the girl. And he could do nothing about it.

He, too, had cursed his body, though it had not developed a disease as Ruby's had. But his pain was intense and the release marvelous when he was able to give his guilt to Jesus, forgive his parents and accept the fact that Jesus had planned that he be male even though his parents had not.

Cursing

Both Ruby and John had been living under a curse of unwantedness. This is a powerful curse resulting from satanic empowerment of thoughts and words of parents or family to the effect that this child is not wanted. Such curses invoke spiritual power against the person, resulting in various kinds of damage to one's spirit, one's emotions and, often, one's body. A frequent result of such prenatal cursing, then, is that the unwanted child responds subconsciously to that curse, and adds curses of his or her own.

I suspect the amount and kind of damage done by such curses relates to the type and level of internal vulnerability of a person. Ruby likely had a physical vulnerability that the enemy could take advantage of. John appeared not to have had such physical vulnerability. He was, however, deeply affected emotionally, suggesting that that was where his greatest vulnerability lay.

The cursing gave the satanic kingdom plenty of ammunition to raise questions in the minds of Ruby and John about whether or not God wanted them to exist or to be a part of God's family.

As I have mentioned, I know from inside myself what a curse of unwantedness is and the self-hate that flows from it. As far back as I can remember, I wallowed in a firm belief that, in spite of much evidence to the contrary, it was normal for bad things to happen to me because I did not belong here. I lived with a Charlie Brown philosophy that it was normal for things to go wrong for me. If anything went right for me, it must be a mistake.

Then one day—I was fifty years old—my wife mentioned to me that there are not nine months between my parents' wedding date and my birthday. This was news to me! But knowing what I had been learning about pre-birth influences, at last the rejection part of my life began to make sense. I forgave my parents and claimed God's power to break any curses on me—both the curses of unwantedness coming from my parents and curses I had put on myself. In addition, I began to claim Scriptures such as Ephesians 1:4 and Jeremiah 1:5 as applying to me. And I got free for the first time from the negative feelings that had plagued me for all of my life.

True, I was conceived under "plan" D, E or F rather than under plan A (God's preferred plan). But *I was wanted by God, even though not by my parents*. Plan A would have made me a bit younger than I am, since my conception would have taken place *after* my parents got married rather than before. But the fact that they got together too soon does not mean that I am a mistake in God's sight. And I can thank God that my parents carried out their intent and did get married and provide a home for me.

Before the World Was Made

Unwantedness, however it comes about, is a lie. Though many feel unwanted, God's perspective is different. He tells us in Ephesians 1:4 that we were wanted before He made the world. He says, "Before I made the world, I chose you." And, if He chose us, He must have planned us. I believe God's words to Jeremiah also apply to us: "Before you were conceived, I knew you; before you were born, I chose you" (see Jeremiah 1:5).

Could it be that God follows His planned genetic rules for every conception? I believe so. But people plan how the conception is to come about. And God can work with a whole alphabet of plans. Even rape, incest and other perversions. Even those who are merely experimenting with sex and get caught. These are obviously not God's plan A; they are the choice of people and God goes along with people's choices. In other words, each conception is ordained by God though carried out by humans. It is God who adds life to the biological partnership that we call conception.

The plan for you was determined long, long ago, before the mountains and the rivers and the oceans and their contents were created. Before the sky and the birds that fill it were created. Long before your parents ever came on the scene, you were lovingly planned by an unimaginably infinite God. Not one of us was a mistake in God's eyes, whatever our parents' attitudes.

There is, therefore, no room for the Charlie Brown attitude. Our coming into existence went right from God's point of view.

Choosing against Our Feelings

For anyone conceived under any plan but A, we face a problem. We do not *feel* as though there was a plan for us. If our parents were not married, it felt yucky in the womb. If we were not the sex our parents wanted, it felt yucky in the womb. If our parents were married but for some reason the conception was inconvenient or unwanted, it felt yucky in the womb. And starting out yucky predicts for most of us a life of feeling yucky about our very existence.

I have worked with many who feel an intense sense of shame, usually reinforced by demons, about their lives. *Shame is feeling bad about who we are, or that we are.* On more than one occasion I have listened as people report that they feel as if they are "just taking up space"—space that really belongs to someone else. They feel they have no right to exist!

The feelings are intense, much worse than the feelings I have had to deal with in my situation. And it usually does not help to say to these people, "Get over it. Believe the truth." The choice to believe the truth seems just too hard for many to imagine.

But it is choice that is the key—choice against feelings, choice to believe the truth. If you are able to assert the necessary willpower to overcome your emotions, Neil Anderson's book *Victory Over the Darkness* (Bethany, 2014) can be a great help. He focuses on the truths about who you are in Christ. If, however, you cannot seem to get where you want to be by simply knowing and believing, then inner healing techniques can help you confront the negative feelings and begin the journey toward healing.

God Has a Plan

After a child's conception, God and the child's mother undertake the process of growing the child. That process is a wonderful partnership. Nor is it purely physical. There is a spiritual side, a side that is God's doing, a side where God reveals His plan. This is a plan that God ordained from eternity.

But God gives free will. And many use that freedom to reject what God has planned for them. Those who accept God's plan and use their free will to follow it discover that it was always there, waiting. It was preordained that there be a plan. Whether or not we accept it is up to us.

God loves us enough that He has a plan for us. And things go well when we assert ourselves to partner with Him in the running of life. When we embrace the plan God chose for us before He made the world, we thwart Satan's plan for us. We know who we are and act like it.

EXERCISE

Many of us feel the pain of being chosen last for a sports team. We remember in elementary school waiting anxiously as the names were called off and the bigger, better-coordinated kids got to join a team while we waited to hear our names. And maybe our names came close to last. Or not at all!

I remember in high school I went out for the baseball team, had a good tryout and was certain I had made the team. Eagerly, I went to view the message board where the names were posted, but to my deep disappointment, my name was not there! I was devastated.

The good news is we all get chosen for God's team! Picture yourself going to the message board and finding your name. Dwell on what it means. Spend some time there, thanking Jesus for the privilege of being chosen to live and play on His team—the team we know will win!

7

Adopted into God's Family

There are numerous stories of orphaned children being adopted into privileged families. Typical of such stories is the child's desolate situation followed by his or her selection by someone who has love and resources to share. Focus is often given to the amazement of the child at being given his or her own room, regular meals, new clothing and the like.

It was not quite like that in our home when quite suddenly a baby girl got to join our family of boys. That is, Sharon did not come to us off the streets or from an orphanage. She came only a few days old and not consciously aware of the fact that she was to grow up in a family of which her biological mother, who was unable to care for her child, was not a part.

Sharon grew up with my parents as her parents and with my two brothers and me as her older brothers. She was tiny when she came and lovable. We adored her. I was fifteen at the time, so I got to care for her a lot until I went off to college and missed most of her growing up years. But she is my little sister to this day, and it has never mattered to us that she had a different biological mother. She was from the start and is to this day an important part of the family, now all grown up and with a family of her own.

She was always special to Dad. And he treated her just as he would have his own biological child. In fact, he probably treated her a bit better than he treated us boys—maybe because she is a girl and he felt she needed more help than us boys; maybe because Dad was older when she came and he had softened quite a bit by that time. But if he treated her better, I was never jealous of her. Nor do I think my brothers were. She was and is one of us. And whatever she needed my parents gave her, just as they did for us boys. No difference, unless there was more favor in her direction.

Feeling Abandoned

I have had the privilege of ministering to several people who were adopted. For many of them, the experience was not a pleasant one emotionally, even though in their heads they usually accepted it as a better option than staying with their birth mothers. The emotional problems tend to center around the feeling that they have been abandoned. They spent nine months before their births in a very intimate relationship with their mothers, but then were cut off from that relationship usually for the rest of their lives.

Feeling abandoned is a very intense emotion. It eats away at an adopted person as very few emotions can do. It is often at the root of behavior that is strange or difficult for the adoptee to understand. Often the person curses him or herself as had Ruby and John. Often there are unexplainable hateful thoughts coming from deep in the person's subconscious toward the biological mother and even toward the adoptive parents.

I once was asked to minister to an eighteen-year-old young man I will call Jack. Though adopted by a couple he and all his friends called wonderful parents, he struggled with a hateful attitude toward them, toward God and toward himself. Jack had been conceived out of wedlock and given up for adoption. He then had lived all his life with a sense of abandonment.

"How could my mother have given me away?" he cried. And now, because of the circumstances of the adoption procedure, there was no way for Jack to meet his birth mother. Not even his adoptive parents knew how to find her.

Jack and I worked through the curses he had put on himself, breaking them in the name of Jesus. I then helped him to understand the turmoil his mother must have experienced as she dealt with the multitude of emotions and the decisions she had to make. Eventually, he was able to forgive his birth mother for her decision and, with the love and power of Jesus, to release both her and God from his anger and to praise God for His provision of a great adoptive family. And, as he gave his anguish to God and gained freedom from his hatefulness, he came to understand the mystery of God's adoption of us in a very special way.

God's Adoption of Us

My parents did not have to adopt Sharon. Nothing was pressing them except that we all wanted a girl in our family.

My parents had hoped for a girl when my next brother was born. But it did not happen. Nor did it happen eight years later when they tried again. That time, they got twin boys (though little Danny only lived about five hours). So they gave up trying to give birth to a girl and adopted one instead.

Nor did the adoptive parents of Jack have to adopt him. It was voluntary on their part, designed to fill a space in their hearts and home that had not been filled naturally. So Jack was a wanted child, chosen to live in a home rather than an orphanage, to experience the love and care of an adoptive family rather than a foster care system run by the government.

There is a sense in which such an adoption is the experience of all of us. We all have sinned and cut ourselves off from our rightful place in God's family. This gave Him every right to abandon us and to leave us in the hands of the parent we had chosen, Satan. But though we were dead (orphaned) in our sin, God voluntarily chose us.

To paraphrase how the apostle John puts it: "See what kind of love the Father has for us that He would call us His children. And so we are" (see 1 John 3:1).

This is adoption. Adoption into the very family of God Himself. Not because we deserved it, but because God of His own free choice reached out to us and adopted us into His "forever" family. Even if we have been enticed by the enemy into believing lies about ourselves and our acceptability to God, the truth is that He is our adopted daddy, and He has chosen us to become full members of His forever family.

Oh, we had to agree to it. We could have run away, as my sister thought of doing from time to time. But if we did not run away, we got to be called God's very own children! This is "way cool."

Now, this has some perks that come along with it. For one thing, we get to inherit as members of the same family as Jesus. Listen to this: God has reserved a priceless inheritance for His children (see 1 Peter 1:4), and, "You are no longer a slave but God's own child. And *since you are his child*, God has made you his heir" (Galatians 4:7 NLT, emphasis added).

I do not claim to know fully what it means to inherit with Christ, but it sure sounds good! It seems as though Jesus ought to get more of a share in any inheritance than we do. And maybe He does. But that is okay. All it says is that we get a share in what He bought for us.

In our family, Sharon gets an equal share with us boys because she came into our family legally by adoption and was given full rights as a sibling, just as if she had come biologically. The same is true for Jack.

The other part of our inheritance is not so nice: We also inherit Jesus' enemies. John says that is why the world hates us. We inherit the hate of the Satan-influenced world around us.

As people hated Jesus, so they will hate us. As they turned against Him and everything He stood for, so they will turn against us if we let it be known who we really are. We may be able to hide our true identity by not mentioning the family we belong to. This, however, is risky since Jesus says in another place, "Whoever denies Me, I will deny" (see Matthew 10:33).

The Arrangements Have Been Made

When Adam sinned, he made us all orphans. This is not how it was supposed to be. We were created to live in an intimate relationship with God. We have a God-shaped vacuum in our hearts, doomed to feeling abandoned until we choose to return to our Maker. This feeling of abandonment is lodged deep in our psyches; people do strange things as expressions of this subconscious damage.

Jesus, then, in working out the details for our adoption, took on Himself our abandonment when He cried out, "My God, my God, why have you abandoned me?" (Matthew 27:46 NLT). Since that awful day, the arrangements have all been made and the only contingency is our agreement—because every adoption must be agreed to by the adoptee, if not at the beginning of the adoption, at least when the person grows to maturity. Many have been the adopted children who at some point in their lives searched until they found their natural parents, and then made a decision either to align with them or to retain their connection with their adoptive parents.

Salvation, then, can be seen as our agreement to accept God's invitation to join His forever family as full members. We give up our feelings of abandonment in favor of the recognition that all the arrangements have been made, and we accept God's offer. From that moment on, God is our proper Father and we His legitimate sons and daughters, accepted and beloved by Him, though hated by the world (see 1 Peter 4:12–13) because of His favor toward us. And now, because He is on our side, who can stand against us?

A student of mine asked if she could have an appointment. I agreed; she came; we talked about a number of things. After a while she interrupted our conversation with the comment, "Gee, you don't act like a professor!" I am not sure what her experience with professors had been, but I did not fit her expectations.

When Jesus came along and proved to His disciples who He was, basically they responded as Peter did after he hauled in the large number of fish at Jesus' bidding. Peter's words were: "Go away from me, Lord! I am a sinful man!" (Luke 5:8 GNT). Peter was uncomfortable in the presence of Jesus. Jesus was too powerful.

Jesus' words and actions distanced Him from the religious establishment. He did not fit their stereotype. He was scary! He did not act like a typical religious leader. This kept people off balance.

Then, when Jesus called His followers "friends" in contrast to "servants" or "slaves" (John 15:14), He presented a model of divine-human interaction quite different from that of the Pharisees and other Jewish leaders.

Are we off balance in the presence of God? One of the things that Jesus was teaching His followers was that when God is near, it is good news, not bad, not fear inspiring. Satan likes to keep our eyes on the bad stuff. This gives him control over people, damaging our relationship with God.

We are invited by Jesus to get close to Him. We are His family members, His sons and daughters.

Do you know who you are?

EXERCISE

When you hear stories about someone who has been adopted, such as the story about my sister, Sharon, what is your reaction? Can you imagine what it would be like to be orphaned or given to another family? If you were adopted, how does that experience affect you today?

Now consider how adoption relates to your standing in Jesus. Do you feel welcomed into the family of God? Do you believe that He really wants you to be in His family? What, if anything, blocks you from enjoying the many benefits of being loved and accepted by your heavenly Father?

8

Redeemed

Humankind turned its back on God. We disobeyed, choosing to follow Satan rather than God. Some angels had done this earlier in eternity and been cast out of heaven forever. Humankind deserved to be banished forever from God's presence as well.

But God did not do so. Why?

I believe the issue is *value*. God values His masterpiece, us. He seems to have a love affair with humans. The angels are only *ministering spirits* (see Hebrews 1:14), there to do God's will and to help His family. We are full *family members*, sons and daughters. We are in on the family affairs. We are part of His forever family. We even inherit with other family members, including Jesus (see Romans 8:17; Hebrews 1:2).

Servants take orders. They do not think for themselves. They obey what their master tells them to do without thinking or questioning.

Humans, on the other hand, are able to think and question. God has given us free will. We can even reject what our Father offers us. Though Adam made a poor choice when he rejected the eternal life God offered him, we can reverse that choice and gain the status Adam rejected.

Our Free Will

God has given us free will. This is His best gift to us, and He wants us to use it wisely and enjoy it. So, again, Satan envies us and tries to steal it from us. And he has been successful, leading many into captivity.

This, then, created a monstrous problem for God. What could He do to rescue His masterpiece? Should He simply write us off as He did with the angels who followed Satan? No, humans are too valuable for that. He must find a way to obey the rules but rescue His beloved humans.

God has established rules for His universe. And both we and He operate within those parameters. Among them are rules of authority in the spirit world. One of these is the rule that whoever we obey "owns" us.

It was humans who gave the creation to Satan. By some rule we do not understand, it must be humans who win it back. According to the apostle Paul, "since by man came death, by Man also came the resurrection of the dead" (1 Corinthians 15:21).

Adam gave the universe away (see Luke 4:6), freely using his authority to represent humankind in giving his allegiance to Satan. To take it back, another Man must use His free will to represent humanity in obeying God. *Whereas the first Adam chose Satan and gave the universe away, the last Adam, through freely choosing obedience to the Creator, took it back.*

And He did it not as God but totally as a human. Jesus laid aside His prerogatives as God (see Philippians 2:6–7), becoming fully human. Though He was still fully God, He never once employed His deity. He lived as God had hoped Adam would, choosing to be totally dependent on Him, thereby defeating the enemy as a human being. As far as we know, only humans were offered salvation—not angels, not animals. Only those made in God's image. Only those beings whose humanity was substantial enough for God Himself in Jesus to enter.

What an amazing thing! What value God has attached to us! Far greater than any value He has attached to even the highest angels. We are precious, valuable to God, in a unique relationship with God—in His eyes worth it.

We are valued above every other of God's creatures. For this reason we have been rescued from the punishment we deserve. That is who we are.

Satan's Loss

Satan and his angels have little or no power and authority except what they can steal from humans. They certainly have no power to redeem, even if they wanted to. Humans can create. We can originate things and innovate. Satan cannot, though he can steal things such as creativity from us.

But Satan and his hosts can deceive people into following him. He can entice us into thinking and doing things that turn us aside from what God wants for us. Suppose, for instance, someone hurts us. God wants us to forgive. Satan wants us to seek revenge. Behaving as Satan wants us to do results in accumulations of emotional and spiritual garbage, giving Satan power over us.

But if we confess and forgive, according to the rules of the universe, God forgives and gives us freedom. These are gifts won by Jesus when He redeemed us from Satan's power. He won our redemption on the cross and in the tomb.

But this redemption is only for humans. The angels—a very important group, serving God's purposes faithfully, without complaint, carrying out God's will without questioning—have not been redeemed. Humans—who are up and down, quite often a disappointment to God—receive His favor. This is the privilege that God gives to those who respond to Him.

Again, Satan loses. He can destroy, but he cannot create. Even if he wanted to, he could not create anything like our redemption. He can only entice, getting people to follow him, so he sets out to win over a person's free will. Satan is strictly limited by God and His rules as operated by those who follow God's way.

Our redemption gives us rights that Satan cannot take away. Our redemption gives us power over Satan, though many humans do not know this and allow themselves to be deceived by him into following his way. When we properly recognize the authority and power our redemption gives us, though, the enemy can only envy us. *He is no match for those who know who they are and act like it.*

Many of Jesus' masterpieces are wonderfully saved but not free. Satan takes advantage of our ignorance to keep in captivity those who do not claim the victory over Satan that our redemption grants us. As humans, we have the right to be free from things like shame, guilt, rage, rejection and a multitude of similar emotions. But if we do not claim that freedom, we remain vulnerable to Satan and his devices.

This vulnerability opens us to habits of low self-worth that generally require therapy to overcome. This therapy has two parts: a human part and a spiritual part. At the human level, psychologists and counselors help us understand and deal with any number of issues.

The spiritual level, however, where we deal with spiritual issues, is not well known; it provides the context for spiritual captivity and is dealt with by using inner healing techniques, such as going back in prayer with Jesus for healing of wounded memories. We also are able to break the power of curses and evil dedications and to deal in depth with the important issue of forgiveness. These and other issues, such as demonization, are spiritual issues that are dealt with in inner healing with the aim of setting captives free.[1]

Jesus wants us to be free (see Galatians 5:1). One of the most precious things He gives is *freedom*. We are those who have been given freedom. Do we know who we are?

EXERCISE

Spend some time reflecting on God's gift of free will. Given the results of our free will (e.g., misuse of political power, misuse of personal power in relationships, choosing to follow Satan in multiple situations), would it have been better if God had not given us free will?

Ponder the chance God took in giving us free will and the great things that have happened because of it.

9

Dignified by the Incarnation

As we have discussed, God could have left us wallowing in our sin, but He did not. Instead He created a plan to redeem us and bring us back from the enemy who had captured us. This plan was not about *doing* something; it was about *being* or *becoming* something. It was an ingenious plan. The Creator would become the creature and take on Himself the punishment for the disobedience of the creature.

By thus taking "creaturehood" on Himself, the rules He had set up would result in freeing the alienated creature to return to his Creator wearing the righteousness of God Himself.

It was a plan that would at once disenfranchise Satan and impute righteousness to the creature. It would also dignify human "creaturehood" in a way no other approach could.

This plan was a "forever plan." The changes it involved would be permanent. The Second Person of the Trinity would *become* a human being. This would be accomplished by God becoming a Man—not requiring that man become God but, in Jesus, *God dignified us by becoming one of us.* To do this, while He remained fully God, "of his own free will he gave up all he had, and took the nature of a servant" (Philippians 2:7 GNT). He became Man to redeem us from His and our enemy.

And when this work was accomplished, God sent the Holy Spirit to comfort and guide those who ask Jesus into their hearts.

The Indwelling Holy Spirit

If you were God, would you entrust humankind with the Holy Spirit?

Imagine what it means to be indwelt by God Himself! Surely God has made a mistake! To fill sinful human beings with His very self? I do not know about you, but I have really struggled with this one. In my self-hating days, I could not imagine how an all-wise God, knowing me inside and out, would take the enormous risk of choosing me to be His. And then that He would choose me as one of the places where He Himself would live (see 1 Corinthians 6:19). Does He not know that I am unworthy and that I will fail Him? If He is so smart, why has He not chosen someone more worthy, more gifted, more likely not to let Him down?

But let's look at the disciples. This should give us a clue concerning the qualifications He expects of those within whom He will live. Were these the kinds of outstanding people that an all-wise God would pick out of all the people on earth to breathe upon, imparting to them His Spirit (see John 20:22)? Given their behavior, it certainly does not look like it. If there was a way to doubt, they found it. If there was a way to misinterpret their Master, they found it. Though they recognized that He was the Messiah, they even felt free to rebuke Him when He did not fit into their concept of how the Messiah should carry out His plans. Are these the kinds of people that the Kingdom of God can be built on?

For reasons that elude human logic, God has chosen people like the apostles and like us with whom to build His Kingdom. This is His plan. And He seems to have no other plan.

The Credit Card

As I have written elsewhere,[1] I like to picture the Holy Spirit as God's "credit card." This picture goes back a few years to when my younger son went off to his university and asked me to put his name on my credit card. This was a boy who had become adept at out-talking his way with us and with siblings and friends. But he promised he would never misuse the credit card. And he is our son. So we added his name to our credit card, and he never misused it.

A credit card represents authority—authority to spend money. My son's name carried no authority with a bank, and if he needed emergency cash, his chances of getting it with his signature were slim. His name on my credit card would, however, assure him of ready cash.

I see God the Father giving His Son such a credit card. We read that Jesus laid aside His prerogatives as God when He came to earth (see Philippians 2:5–7). We know from the amazement of the people of His hometown, Nazareth, that when He began to do miracles, He did no mighty works before His baptism. Then, at His baptism, the Holy Spirit came upon Him (see Luke 3:21–22), and He began to do miraculous things. God the Father had given Jesus the "credit card" with the Father's name at the top and Jesus' name under it. Only then did Jesus have the authority to teach and to do mighty works, demonstrating both God's love and who man is supposed to be.

You have the "credit card." What will you do with it?

Imitate Jesus

Jesus has become one of us—God become man. An important reason for Him to become a man is so that we can learn to be like Him. We are to learn to love as He loves, to forgive as He forgives—in short, to be like Jesus. As the apostle Paul said, "For to me, to live is Christ" (Philippians 1:21). Jesus became one of us so we would become like Him.

Jesus was the perfect example for us. What was His ego like? He knew who He was. And He had confidence in the Father, even to the point of paying the ultimate sacrifice to rescue His beloved masterpiece—us.

EXERCISE

Ponder what Jesus' taking on human flesh, rather than coming in some other form, means. Could He have come in some other form? Or not come at all?

What would have been communicated if He had come solely as God rather than as God incarnate: a Man? How does the Holy Spirit figure in this?

10

The Apostle Peter

I f I didn't have confidence in you, you wouldn't be in the game." These were the words of my baseball coach who had called time out to encourage a very discouraged batter on the way to his fifth strikeout in a row! It was my junior year in college, and we were playing our archrivals against their ace pitcher. He was a good pitcher. But I was one of our better hitters, and I should have been able to hit off him.

"Time out!" called our coach. As he came running to me in the batter's box, I thought, *He's going to take me out of the game.* Indeed, I wanted him to take me out. I had given up on myself. But his words were words of affirmation.

"Close your eyes," he said, "stand on your head, get down on your knees, do something you've never done before, but *hit the ball*! If I didn't have confidence in you, you wouldn't be in the game."

This left me mentally reeling. But I hit the ball off the left field fence.

I heard God that day in the affirming words of a college coach, in the trivial experience of a baseball game.

I believe Peter had this kind of experience when His coach, Jesus, allowed him back into His discipleship group. "Do you love Me?" Jesus asked, reminding Peter of the day he had quit, but accepting Peter's confession and restoring him. Peter never forgot those words of restoration and became a giant in the early Church.

Incidentally, our baseball team faced the same pitcher the following year, my senior year. My coach's words were still fresh in my ears. We got only two hits off him, and I had both—a single and a home run. We lost the game—but I won.

Who are you? You have come to Christ for life. You are invited to serve. You trust Him and God trusts you. You probably fail Him a lot—all of us do. But He never gives up on you. He has confidence in you.

Peter's Story

My story is much less important than Peter's. Indeed, it may only be significant because it is mine and, therefore, important to me. But there is a point at which all of our stories resemble each other and convey a similar message. God does not give up on us.

Satan must get frustrated at times. Peter would have been one who frustrated him. I picture Peter as a rough, tough fisherman, making his living by challenging the water and the wind.

If he was like most fishermen, his language would have been salty. This comes out toward the end of Jesus' life when Peter cursed and swore he was not one of Jesus' men (see Matthew 26:69–75). We could guess that satanic spirits had claimed Peter and expected him to work for Satan's side within the small band of Jesus' followers who had pledged themselves to Him.

Satan certainly knew who Peter was. I am not sure Peter knew. What Peter knew was that he was a fisherman (see Matthew 4:18), that he was passionately dedicated to Jesus (see Matthew 16:16–19, 22–23; John 18:10), that he was sure Jesus was the Messiah (see Matthew 16:16–19), that he was one of Jesus' best friends and many other such things.

But when the going got tough, he denied his relationship with Jesus (see John 18:15–18, 25–27). The enemy got Peter big time. Peter's loyalty was tested, and he failed. But, fortunately, the story does not end with a victory for Satan. The trust Jesus put in Peter paid off.

Hidden Potential

It was not predictable that Jesus would choose Peter (or any of them, truly) to be His disciple. Peter was a fisherman, an unlikely candidate to become one who would challenge the religious establishment. He was impulsive, outspoken and crude; yet something attracted him to Jesus. And that attraction generated a fierce loyalty and protectiveness toward Jesus that eventually cost him his life—but not before he became the fearless leader of the early Christian movement.

Did Jesus see potential in Peter? Or did Jesus choose Peter mostly because Peter chose Jesus?

The situation was confusing. Peter had given himself to Jesus and His cause. He had even pledged his life to Jesus—to the death! (see Matthew 26:35). His commitment was total, except for his fear that threw him right into Satan's arms at the time when Jesus needed Peter's support the most.

But those denials were not the final chapter.

Jesus knew Peter well. Though Peter's denials were a disappointment, Jesus knew that, empowered by the Holy Spirit, Peter could become Jesus' lead disciple. "Do you love Me more than My other disciples do?" (see John 21:15–17).

"I have confidence in you, Peter. Do you trust yourself?" Three times Peter denied Jesus, three times he needed to affirm his commitment. This was a broken disciple facing his best friend—as I had once faced my baseball coach and found out that he had not given up on me. That event, more than any other in my growing-up days, made a man of me. I met my coach years later and my word to him was, "I heard God that day, and my life was never the same again."

Satan's Defeat

That day on the baseball diamond Satan was happy that I had failed in all my previous attempts. He was especially happy that I took the event so seriously. It was, after all, only a game—except for a boy who was trying to prove his manhood, always trying to prove himself to his dad, and to himself.

Now the stakes are higher. I have given myself to God. And the prize is not just a game. We are at war and the enemy does not let up. He knows who we are. Do we?

In spite of Peter's failures, Jesus had confidence in him, and Peter came to be a giant in the early Church. Though he was a Galilean with little prospect of acceptance, Peter led a massive turning to Christ in Jerusalem.

And the enemy lost.

Peter discovered who he could be. So did I. So can you.

EXERCISE

Ponder one or more experiences in your life when you felt inadequate but someone encouraged you. Let yourself feel the trust God has in you: "If I didn't have confidence in you, you wouldn't be in the game."

11

Spiritual Warfare

We live in warfare. God is at war with Satan. Both sides have millions of invisible beings carrying out their will. Just as God empowers His people to carry out His will, so Satan empowers his followers to support his side. We are to be warriors with God.

Satan and his dark angels work full-time to mess up God's plans and His people. They are agents of temptation and advocates of interpersonal conflict. They are experts of deceit, liars from the beginning, just as committed to evil as God is to good.

These are our enemies, working largely in secret to thwart God's program and destroy His people.

It soon becomes obvious, then, that an important part of our identity is to see ourselves as warriors. We are to recognize that we are involved in a cosmic war against Satan and all of his troops. This is a spiritual war, but humans are the prize. Satan's aim is to gain the allegiance of God's most precious creatures who will then use the gift of free will to follow him.

We who have used our God-given free will to choose God's side are warriors for Him; however, many of those God has called to fight for Him are sitting on the sidelines. Either they are in the war but afraid, and thus compromised so that they do not participate in the fighting, or they do not recognize that we are at war. They may be so into the relational and love parts of our faith that they think that is all there is. Our relationship with Christ is indeed crucial, but we have the responsibility to serve Jesus' cause as well as to enjoy that relationship.

Those who are not participating in the war may be spiritually free, but they do not recognize that there is more to Christianity than they are experiencing. Satan is smart enough to leave these people pretty much alone, lest they wake up and become a threat to him. Satan works on them but keeps them ignorant, no threat to him and his strategies.

I was once in that group, as is most of the Church today. I did little to bother Satan, and he did little that was obvious enough for me to recognize that he was behind it.

If we miss the war going on around us, we will likely take a secular approach to all of life's problems. We will do church regularly, pray regularly, practice love and other "Christian behavior" and call ourselves Christians. And so we are. And so are our fellow church members. But Satan works in the background, participating in events such as sickness, accidents and misfortunes that turn us to thoughts of anger, revenge and shame or even the contemplation of suicide—and we fail to recognize that we are in a war with a powerful enemy. A major result of Satan's activity is to turn us against ourselves in self-hatred and low self-image.

We Are at War

We are at war, whether or not we recognize it. And our enemy is very active in keeping us from discovering who we are supposed to be.

The apostle Paul puts it this way: "For we do not wrestle against flesh and blood, but against principalities, against powers, against the rulers of the darkness of this age, against spiritual hosts of wickedness in the heavenly places" (Ephesians 6:12).

This is warfare language. Paul saw himself as a warrior, charged with joining his Master in fighting the enemy. He was joined in partnership with Jesus in spiritual warfare.

So we, like Paul, are at war as God's partners, enlisted by God to fight Satan's partners. And Satan knows that we can defeat him if we ever learn to use the power God gives us. We are a threat to Satan if we ever find out who we are and start acting like it.

The battle is fought on our turf. Fighting goes on in the heavenlies, but our responsibility is to defeat the enemy in our context. There seems to be a principle that Satan is to be defeated by us humans, on our turf. Romans 16:20 puts it this way: "The God of peace will crush Satan under *your* feet" (emphasis added).

Jesus did His part as a human empowered by the Holy Spirit. We are to do our part as Holy Spirit–filled humans. We have infinitely more power than Satan does—as our champion, Jesus, demonstrated. But we must learn how and when to use it.

Put On the Armor

In preparation for meeting Satan in battle, we are to gird ourselves with the armor of God. Paul makes this clear: "Therefore take up the whole armor of God, that you may be able to withstand in the evil day, and having done all, to stand" (Ephesians 6:13).

He goes on to specify the various parts of armor we are to put on. We are to gird our waists with truth, put on the breastplate of righteousness, cover our feet with the preparation of the gospel of peace, and:

> Above all, [take] the shield of faith with which you will be able to quench all the fiery darts of the wicked one. And take the helmet of salvation, and the sword of the Spirit, which is the word of God; praying always with all prayer and supplication in the Spirit.
>
> Ephesians 6:16–18

These are warfare words, designed to call us to action. We are to be ready at all times to engage our enemy's troops. He does not rest. He is relentless in his attacks. We must be on our guard at all times.

Jesus was always on guard. He knew who He was and how to use His power to defeat the enemy and show His love to those the enemy was tormenting. We are expected by God to do likewise.

Being Constantly On Guard

Paul alerts us to the fact that our enemy never sleeps. He is always looking to influence the most precious thing God has given us—our free will—and thus to gain partners to fight against God.

When humans follow the enemy or ignore him, they give victories to the enemy. Often these victories are in the area of self-worth, where Satan manipulates circumstances to turn God's people against themselves.

Many people who have been given the power to defeat Satan either ignore their calling to fight Satan or refuse to engage him. Many who are alerted to the fact that we are at war refuse to get involved because they would not know what to do if things got out of hand. They have not been taught about the connection between who we are and what we are called to do. Our position in Christ is not simply a privilege; it carries with it a responsibility—to join the war.

We are rarely taught in our institutions about the warfare part of our faith. Rare indeed are the ministerial training programs where spiritual warfare is dealt with. And this lack carries into the preaching and teaching parts of church ministry. Thus, the fear exists that we might not be able to handle a demonic outbreak should one occur.

But according to our Scriptures, spiritual warfare is part of what our individual and church lives are all about. And I believe God expects it to be a vital part of our self-image. Our God is a warring God; we are expected to be a warring people.

Jesus used His power to demonstrate His love. We should imitate Jesus' behavior. There are many people in our circles who are afflicted by our enemy and whom God wants us to heal and deliver from demons.[1]

Let's be warriors for Jesus.

EXERCISE

As our exercise for this chapter, I would like you to seek out occasions in the New Testament where spiritual warfare is practiced or demonstrated.

12

Temples of the Holy Spirit

Surely you know that you are God's temple and that God's
Spirit lives in you! . . . For God's temple is holy, and you
yourselves are his temple.

1 Corinthians 3:16–17 GNT

Temples are holy places where God lives among His
people. Again, God's choice is to live with His people
rather than in some distant place, inaccessible to humans.

The apostle Paul points out the consistent message that
God Himself chooses to be close rather than distant, living
inside of us rather than outside of us. No angel or animal
can claim this.

Those of us in the Western world are not usually talking or thinking about temples. But there are places both
in the past and in the present where temples are a really
big deal. A temple signifies the place where people meet
God: a sacred place, a holy place.

The Temple was vitally important in orthodox Judaism in Jesus' day; so revered was it that many worshiped it. Thus, when Jesus said, "Tear down this Temple, and in three days I will build it again" (John 2:19 GNT), and when He told the Pharisees that Someone in their midst was greater than the Temple (see Matthew 12:6), and when He chased out of the Temple those doing commerce there (see John 2:13–16), the religious leaders felt that Jesus was behaving heretically.

Indeed, one of the accusations they made during Jesus' trial was that He did not honor the Temple. Speaking against the Temple was, in the minds of Jewish leaders, desecrating the Law and, therefore, worthy of death.

Forms and Meanings

How did this happen? How did the legalistic arm of the Jewish community—the Pharisees—come to revere the Temple to this extent?

Because of the meaning they assigned to it. Within cultures, communities assign certain meanings to the beliefs and practices that are important to them. These beliefs and practices, which are called *forms* in culture studies, are things like words, rituals, religious doctrines and every other cultural entity whether concrete or theoretical. The *forms* are the entities themselves; the *meanings* are the interpretations people give them. Forms in this sense are structural; meanings are personal—the meanings belong to the persons who assign them.

In every culture, every time we speak or write, we have meanings we are trying to get across. And those meanings, especially if they refer to religious forms, often carry strong emotional content. The Jews throughout their history were strongly committed to the meaning they attached to the Temple.

This was, in part, because God Himself had instituted the Temple as the place where His people would meet with Him. But over the generations that followed, as the Jewish culture itself changed, so did the meanings of its religious forms. The Temple, to the strictest Jews, had morphed from a place where worship took place into a building that was itself worthy of worship. It was the latter meaning that Jesus was tackling.

Jesus was challenging the Pharisees concerning their religion. To Jesus, the cultural thing called *religion* was not what it was all about. Jesus did not intend to bring another religion into a world already full of religions. His was a message about a relationship with the God of the universe—a relationship between free moral agents that is personal, not institutional. So, when Jesus challenged their perceptions of the Temple, He was challenging the institution (the cultural form) called *Judaism* in order to get at the relational essence (the true meaning) of what He sought to bring.

He said, "My house is a house of prayer"—a relational (meaning) thing, not simply an institutional (form) thing (see Luke 19:46). It was the Jews who turned the relationship into an institution, complete with rules and regulations, sacred times and places, even customs that were expected to work like magic and taboos that if broken would bring punishment.

Jesus' view was a view that puts persons first; whatever is done institutionally is secondary to the needs of persons.

God is a loving Father, a charitable one who encourages His children—not the legalistic judge who stands with a whip in His hand waiting for His child to make a mistake.

Yes, this God has standards that He holds His children to. But these standards are in place to benefit people, not to enslave them. And it is always the relationship—not the rules—that governs the interaction between God and His children.

The Results for Relationship

What does this do for our relationship? Everything!

To love is to do what is best for the object of the love. For God to love His precious children, He continually does what is best for us as persons, even if it does not square with the expectations of those who run the institutions, who apply misguided meanings to God-given forms.

A woman was brought to Jesus having been caught in the act of adultery (see John 8:3). What would Jesus do? The Scriptures themselves prescribed that she be stoned. She knew what the penalty should be. The keepers of the institution, devoid of concern for relationship, put the question to Jesus. Must she not be stoned? Does our institution not demand but one recourse?

So, in their minds, Jesus had to choose between His ethic of mercy and their understanding of the rules. If He judged with mercy and let the woman go untouched, He could be seen as endorsing a pretty serious sin. If He judged with legalism and said she must be stoned, He could be seen as a hypocrite who only talked about—not practiced—love and mercy. They were sure they had Him.

For these legalists, the meaning they had applied to the form of Scripture allowed no options. *Of course He must let her be stoned,* they thought. *And He will forevermore be discredited.*

But, no. Jesus outwitted them. While perfectly fulfilling the Law, He also accepted a wounded woman. He called off the men, revealing their hypocrisy in the process. He chose to fulfill the spirit of the Law, not through the rules they had imposed upon it but through relationship, choosing the person rather than religion. This is our God.

Interesting. And because He fulfilled the Law through relationship rather than legalism, He was accused of heresy. Were not these rules given to them by God? Yes, in one generation. But this was another generation, and when the true meaning got lost in that latter generation, there needed to be change to get back to the proper meaning.

God condemned the practice of worshiping the Temple, and Jesus prophesied its destruction. The same thing had happened with the brass snake in the wilderness (see Numbers 21:9; John 3:14). The thing God instituted in one generation for healing became an object of worship in another generation. He condemned the practice because the meaning had been changed, and He removed the forms from their midst.

Go for Meaning

What is the relevance of all of this to us? Look for the meanings. Unlike the Jews of Jesus' day who lost the true meaning of their faith in their reverence for the Temple, we fix our eyes and our allegiance on Jesus, "the author and finisher of our faith" (Hebrews 12:2).

Our meanings are in our relationship with Jesus, not in the religious rituals, no matter how meaningful they may be.

Who are we? We are the ones who follow Jesus all the way—the ones who are known by our faithfulness to Him.

We have a God who is on our side. That is who we are.

EXERCISE

Go back to our first exercise with the mirror (found in the Introduction) and grade yourself. How are you doing in developing a positive attitude toward yourself? Can you, as God's masterpiece, confront the enemy?

Think of several more positive things you can say to yourself and practice them.

13

Able to Create Others

At the time of writing, my wife and I can claim fifteen grandchildren. As our four children were growing up, I do not remember thinking about what an inestimable privilege it is to be able to create brand-new beings who will live for eternity. Oh, my wife and I marveled over the miracle of each birth and the joy of participating in their lives as they grew through the various stages of childhood and into adulthood. But the privilege, the inestimable privilege that God has given us to co-create with Him, has only really hit me as I enjoy our fifteen grandchildren and the fifteen (at last count) great-grandchildren they have brought into the world.

Our grandchildren and great-grandchildren are very special. Perhaps it is because we are not so busy taking care of them that we have time to savor the joy of watching them grow up. We love to have birthday parties for them. Since most of them live near enough to come to our house regularly, we have get-togethers to celebrate one or more birthdays just about every month.

They invade our house. Each of them has one or more special places they like to go to—rooms with games and DVD players become populated by groups of kids of similar ages. The three-year-olds are especially fond of movies at their level, and the adults who are not playing cards usually watch along with them.

And as I sit there enjoying whatever group I am with, I think, *These kids are not only in their parents' image, they are in God's image.* They will live forever, and we with them forever with God. Children are not just a temporary thing, a stage in our lives while we take care of them and get them launched into adulthood. Children and grandchildren are forever, creations of a partnership between God and their parents.

Satan Does Not Like Children

As we would expect, our enemy, Satan, does not like it that we can create beings in God's image. He is jealous of us and of them. I believe Satan is sterile, unable to create anything, certainly not children who will live forever. God has given that privilege to only one type of being in the universe as far as we know—us.

So Satan does his dead-level best to mess these kids up. He brings temptation after temptation their way, especially as they grow into adolescence. Sexual temptations are his favorites, since he is so put out that God has made us sexual beings. Indeed, this is probably the major area in which he tempts adults as well, seeking to get us to bring unwanted children into existence or to use sex to hurt and abuse each other. Satan's ways are devious, but his desire to get us to misuse the privilege of sexuality is clear.

Satan Does Not Like Women Either

I have asked demons on a few occasions why they seem to be so hard on women. Their consistent answer is something like this: "Because they give life"—said with a sneer. If there is anything Satan dislikes more than our reproductive capacity, it may be our very life. As Jesus said, the devil seeks to "kill and destroy" (John 10:10 NLT). And those who give life are a primary target.

To torment women, our enemy has two strong allies: society and men. As I pointed out in chapter 1, social standards are hard on women. In Western societies comes the constant message that a given woman's body is not the right size or shape, or that a woman is not living up to society's standards for social behavior or motherhood or homemaking or career or . . . It feels as though one can never do it right. In other societies, women are often looked down on, belittled and dishonored in startling ways. Satan is active in encouraging low self-esteem in women through damaging social standards.

Then there are the problems some men create for women. Because women wield incredible power through the granting or withholding of sexual favors, some men are afraid of women. Mothers have great power over sons as they grow up; wives and lovers have great influence over adult men through their sex drives.

In reaction, some men use their greater mobility and

freedom to oppress women. In doing so, these men are siding with Satan in his attempts to harm them.

Many men, especially godly men, do not treat women in this way. And God has blessed women with the ability, even under difficult, sometimes harsh circumstances, to survive, thrive and create. Satan has met his match in women! In spite of the ways in which society and men side with the enemy to damage women, most do very well, especially in their God-given task to conceive and carry infants inside them and to nurture them before birth (hopefully with male assistance after). The creation of new life is a privilege God has given His highest creation—with women playing the major role. If I were Satan, I would be jealous, too!

Partnership

Regarding children, as in many other areas of life, God chooses to work in partnership with humans. I believe God has made a rule for Himself that in human affairs He ordinarily works with a human partner.

Co-creation is partnering with God to make brand-new beings, beings who will live forever. We create, with God, beings that have never existed previously. And He does not do it without our cooperation.

This is amazing! Without Him we cannot make new beings. Without us He will not make new beings. We have to do our part or it does not happen.

We get to partner with God Himself. What an inestimable privilege! Angels cannot participate in co-creation, but we can. Lift your heads, partners with God.

Do you know who you are?

EXERCISE

Keep working with the mirror. This time focus on the marvel of the process that you and God went through as you grew from a helpless baby to an adult. Let loose your memories to focus on the care and protection God has given you over the years, especially in experiences that could easily have been disastrous if they had gone the wrong way.

Focus on the fact that God protects you because He values and loves you. Talk to that person in the mirror about your value to God and to yourself.

14

Doing the Stuff

Jesus was a healer. He showed His love to those created in God's image in many ways, one of which was to heal. And because we have the privilege of being like Him, we get to be healers. That is part of who we are.

Unfortunately, though we gladly accept His healing, few of us have been taught that we are to be healers. We assume that Jesus could heal because He never stopped being God. But we forget that He "emptied himself, by taking the form of a servant" (Philippians 2:7 ESV) and lived on this earth as a man, showing us what we are expected to be. Working as a man, then, under the leading of the Holy Spirit, Jesus showed us that as He is a healer, so we are to be healers.

In January 1982 we, the faculty of the School of World Mission, started a course called Signs, Wonders and Church Growth at Fuller Seminary where I was teaching. We had invited a pastor named John Wimber to teach us the things he and his church were learning about healing and deliverance from demons.

John had come from an evangelical, non-Pentecostal background as most of us had, but God had led him into a healing and deliverance ministry. I was especially interested since the Nigerian church leaders I had worked with as a missionary identified problems with demons as their greatest concern, and I had not known how to help them.

In class John would lecture for a while, then close his book and say, "Now, let's do the stuff." By this he meant, "It's time for ministry." Then he would ask the Holy Spirit to come and show whom He would like to heal or deliver from demons. The Holy Spirit would come and first identify whom He wanted to heal; then, at either Wimber's or a student's command of healing, Jesus would heal that person.

As the course went on, we began to learn, first, that God loves to heal and, then, how we can partner with God to bring healing and deliverance from demons. Wimber taught us that we all could be healers and deliverers; we all could "do the stuff."

And learning that we all could work with Jesus to free people changed my life. I discovered that I could work with Jesus in a healing ministry and began to practice. This is now an important part of who I am.

Satan is especially upset if we start doing the works Jesus promised we would do (see John 14:12). Satan's best strategy is to keep us ignorant that we are healers. If we begin using God's power as Jesus did, the enemy is in big trouble. And he knows it. Jesus has declared war against Satan's works, and He wants us to join Him.

In the use of God's power we need to know who we really are, who God is and what authority and power God wants to wield through us. To this end He gives us (in partnership) authority and power to cast out demons and to heal in His name (see Luke 9:1). We are also given the power to bless and to protect.

I think it noteworthy that Jesus *did not pray* for people to be healed or delivered; He *commanded* it. He acted as if He owned the place. And I believe He wants us to join Him in bold partnership because it is our war as well as His.

This is one of the main things Wimber taught. We are not to beg God to do something He really wants to do. Our enemy cannot stand against "Jesus people"—people to whom Jesus has given His power—if we exercise our right to heal and deliver. The higher-level cosmic demons, the principalities and powers spoken of in Ephesians 6, may have more power than the ground-level spirits in their efforts to keep us in bondage, but none has the power of Jesus and His followers.

How Much Power Do You Carry?

I once ministered to a woman who had an interesting spiritual gift. She could see how much power any person carried. This woman told me and the team working with me that every one of us carries a certain amount of spiritual power. She noted that certain types of people carry a lot of power, while other types carry less, sometimes much less. One of the reasons she had come to Christ was the fact that Christians tend to carry a lot of power. Likely she was jealous of those with power and decided to join them.

Demons can see this power as well and walk carefully to avoid confrontation, since they carry very little power. They usually do not have a big problem keeping even high-powered Christians from using their power. They get a lot of help from our culture, which considers demons to be mythical.

On our side, then, we need to educate our people concerning what demons are and how they work. We need to help people recognize that we can defeat demons by using the power that is ours.

This is key to our protection. If negative things are going on around us, we can claim Jesus' presence and protection. I have developed a habit of confronting suspicious events by saying, "If this is the enemy, stop it." I often do not know if Satan is behind given events, so I say *if*. Whenever I assert my authority in this way, things have changed approximately half the time.

Satan is always ready to push events and conversations in a negative direction, and he does this quietly so that most people do not even recognize what is happening. Even what we call accidents are often instigated by satanic beings. Satan and his helpers are very present and very active in the human context.

I suspect that people who seem to be just naturally negative are influenced by Satan. I know a person who can turn any conversation negative. She is hard to be around. You can go to her with exciting good news, and within a few minutes you have descended into gloom and doom. Satan loves it!

Most people are not that extreme, thank God! But we need to be aware and protect ourselves from Satan's influence in whatever form it might come. Our God is greater than all the negativity and all the unexplained events. He is always there and willing to work in partnership with us to thwart the enemy's influence in larger and smaller events.

I believe that Jesus wants us to bring healing to those who are hurting—whether emotional healing or physical healing or casting out demons. That is who we are supposed to be—healers.

Walking in Jesus' Authority

Janice was an adult living with emotional wounds that compromised just about all she did. She had grown up with an abusive father who beat her regularly for reasons she seldom understood. She came to me in hopes that I, with Jesus, could bring healing at the deepest level.

We focused on her father and his roughness with his daughter. I asked her to go back in her memory and to picture herself in one of the beatings she experienced. Janice did that, picturing herself curled up in a corner of the room taking a beating. And the tears came.

Then I simply asked, "Where is Jesus?"

Janice saw Jesus in her picture. She pictured the truth: Jesus *was* there. He knew what was happening. He showed her that He was there and on her side, helping her. Janice softened and was able to forgive her father, bringing healing.

When Jesus sent His followers out into the villages, He "gave them power and authority over all demons, and to cure diseases" (Luke 9:1). The disciples were empowered.

That is who they were, and I believe those words apply to us as well.

Unfortunately, our Christianity has become powerless; we forget that healing and deliverance were an important part of our Lord's ministry, and that He passed along that part as well as the important love and relationship part. So, being the people that He intended for us to be includes the power part. Satan and demons are real; we Jesus-followers are the ones Jesus has commissioned to use His power to free people.

I was brought up in secular Christianity and thought that was what Christian life was to be. I had, however, a sneaking suspicion that this was not all there was to our faith. This continued until I listened to John Wimber. I first watched him as he appropriated the power Jesus promised us. Then I stepped out daringly and began to see God work in power through me. It changed my life and did wonders for my self-image. I got to feel as though I was important and more orthodox theologically than I had ever been. And more normal.

Satan's Tactics

In order to determine who we are, then, it is helpful to know who our enemy is and what he does. First of all we need to know that he seeks to take the Kingdom away from God. When God created man and gave the Kingdom to him, this angered Satan; along with our being made in God's likeness, this probably is a key reason he hates humans so much.

So, Satan does his level best to disrupt human life. He challenged human life and lost at the cross and the tomb. Satan cannot beat God, so he picks on God's masterpiece: us.

There are wars, there are murders, there is sexual perversion, there is human trafficking, there is dishonesty and corruption in high places. Is it not clear that Satan is alive and well and doing his work in the human context?

Satan is jealous of humans. He wants us to believe we are nothing, insignificant, powerless. When we hang our heads and put ourselves down, we agree with Satan that we are what Satan says we are rather than what God says we are. And when we agree with Satan, we become what he says we are: powerless.

Do you know that you are to be a healer? That is part of who you are.

You are all the things God says you are and none of the things Satan says you are. This book is intended to point you to these things. Live in them.

EXERCISE

I would like you to learn to heal. Find those who need healing and practice commanding the condition to be healed. You may not be successful on the first tries, but never give up.

When I started, I focused on bringing healing from headaches. With my focus on "little things," I found that about thirty percent of the people I prayed for got relief—though not always complete healing.

As I continued, I found that my record with emotional problems was much better, especially when I used an inner healing approach. My theory is that each of us is more gifted in certain areas, and that is why there is more success in that area. Keep working with those who need healing and find the area in which you are particularly gifted.

15

Yoked to Jesus

A major issue in addressing our self-image is the nature of our relationship to Jesus. Jesus spent the years of His ministry living with and teaching twelve disciples. In working with them, He said and did some startling things. None was more startling than the position Jesus gave to these disciples in relation to Him and to God's Kingdom.

Jesus' disciples were Galileans—all but one of them (Judas). Galileans were disrespected throughout Israel, looked down on, not trusted. "Can anything good come out of Nazareth?" (John 1:46), people asked rhetorically, referring to one of its towns. But with this bunch Jesus turned the world upside down—because they partnered with Him. They were junior partners, to be sure, but partners nevertheless. Jesus did not turn the world upside down by Himself.

At one point Jesus used the analogy of a farmer and his oxen. The custom was to have two oxen pulling the plow. One ox was a strong ox, the other a weaker one—perhaps an apprentice or an older ox. The job of the weaker ox was to walk half a step behind the stronger one. Most of the weight, then, was pulled by the stronger ox, less by the weaker one—unless he got out of step and began to get ahead of the stronger one. The oxen were in partnership, but they were expected to pull different proportions of the load. Theoretically, the farmers could have used a single ox. But they did not.

This is the analogy Jesus had in mind when He said, "Take My yoke upon you and learn from Me; apprentice to Me; enter into partnership with Me. The yoke won't be too much for you" (see Matthew 11:29).

The work will not get done unless both oxen are in the yoke and pulling according to their strengths. So it is with Jesus and His disciples. No work gets done unless the junior partner is in the yoke and engaged. We are to serve Jesus—but freely, as friends, not as slaves. Jesus said as much when He said, "I don't call you slaves; I call you friends, partners" (see John 15:15). We are in on the plans God has made. The Kingdom is ours as well as His. So we pull the load with Him, but we are also owners (partners), not merely servants.

Can God Do Anything He Wants?

Many of us have neglected a major part of what God intends for us. We have spent a lot of energy learning who God is. We have studied the Scriptures diligently to find out all we can about God. This is good. We need to learn as much as possible about God. We have learned about His character and His characteristics. He is righteous and good. He is omnipotent, omnipresent, omniscient.

But I think we have tended to overdo it in at least one area. We have tended to misconstrue His omnipotence. We have assumed that omnipotence means that He can do anything He wants to do at any time He wants to do it.

If this is true, He really does not need us. If this is true, prayer, worship, fasting, the Lord's Supper, baptism and any other rituals we do are just religious observances (forms) with little or no relationship to the realities of life around us! If He can do whatever whenever, what we do makes no difference unless it be for us to grow in our faith and to bring a few others into saving faith. Everything belongs to Him, and we are just along for the ride until He decides to wrap things up.

This misses the fact that God seems to have put certain limits on Himself. Could it be that there are things God cannot do?

We know He has given humans free will. Might the gift of free will for His creatures result in limitations on our Creator? Or has He given us something that He constantly interferes with?

I believe that God has made rules for Himself. He is omnipotent, omniscient and omnipresent, yes. He cannot be limited by anything outside Himself. But He can make rules for Himself that result in certain limits on Him from inside. We have to go no further than 2 Peter 3:9 to learn that He does not always get His way on earth: "The Lord is not slack concerning His promise, as some count slackness, but is longsuffering toward us, not willing that any should perish but that all should come to repentance." He wants all people to come to Him. But, according to this verse, that will not happen. Likewise, if God always gets His way, why would Jesus pray that His Kingdom should come, His will be done on earth as in heaven (see Matthew 6:10)?

God does not want people to go to hell. But we see in Scripture that many people will go to hell, against God's will. They go to hell because of their choices, not because God has ordained it. Human free will is very real. It is not a sham.

Partnership

I believe Scripture shows us some of the rules God has made for Himself (perhaps not all of them). But the one I want to talk about here is a major one. It concerns partnership. The rule says this: *God chooses to do His work in the human arena mainly in cooperation (yoked) with a human partner.* Or, to put it the other way around: *God regularly withholds things He wants to do in the human arena until humans get involved in bringing it about.*

So, what happens on earth is in major ways predicated upon what humans decide it to be. God's will is constant; the part of the operation that is unpredictable is that of the human partners.

There are many obvious examples in Scripture and in life. The first that I will mention is *salvation. God will not save us unless we choose to relate to Him.* He will not save us against our will. God is always willing and anxious for people to come to Him. Salvation occurs when a person uses his or her free will to line up with God's. God says, "Come to me, all of you who are tired from carrying heavy loads, and I will give you rest" (Matthew

11:28 GNT). His is an open invitation, but no one gets in unless we, the junior partners, make the choice to come to Him.

A second example is *forgiveness. God says He will not forgive us unless we ask Him to* (see 1 John 1:9). And, in addition, according to Matthew 6:14–15, His forgiveness of us is also dependent upon our forgiving others. This is scary. But the Senior Partner has made a rule here both for Himself and for us, the junior partners.

A third example is *prayer.* Though God is good and gives us many things we do not ask for, *He regularly withholds things from us until we ask Him for them.* Otherwise, what is prayer about? God already knows what we need and what we want, but He often waits for us to ask Him. In addition, prayer is an act of war. What we take to God establishes our position on God's side against the enemy. Prayer is the activity of junior partners shouldering our part of the load in recognition of the fact that God works in partnership with His people.

A fourth area, similar to prayer, is *healing.* Though God regularly heals indirectly through medicine and doctors, *He rarely, if ever, heals directly unless we open ourselves to Him in faith*, claiming the authority of the junior partner to partner with God to bring about His will. The junior partner has the authority to command healing as Jesus did.

Are you yoked with Jesus? We have the inestimable privilege of being able to choose to partner with Jesus and see His will be done. That is who we are.

---EXERCISE--

Picture oxen yoked together. Now picture yourself with Jesus pulling one side of the yoke and you a half step behind Him. Let yourself ponder what this means if you fail to carry out your part. Then picture yourself carrying out your part properly.

16

Partnering with Jesus

God had a plan for the humans He had made. They were to share authority over the created universe with Him. God created Adam and Eve to fill the earth and subdue it (see Genesis 1:26–30).

God had one condition for them: They needed to work *with* Him, not independently from Him. They were to be partners in running the world—God and humans yoked together, working with each other. Though Adam and Eve failed to carry out their part of the deal by disobeying God and partnering with Satan, the partnership rule still held.

It was in partnership with Noah that God devised a way to rescue humanity when they were untrue to the partnership. He then partnered with Abraham to create a people of God. He partnered with Joseph to rescue God's people from famine. He partnered with Moses to rescue God's people from oppression—after He had partnered with Moses' mother to hide the child and with Pharaoh's daughter to raise him.

God then partnered with Joshua to claim the Promised Land. He partnered with the judges (e.g., Gideon), the prophets (e.g., Samuel, Elijah, Isaiah), the kings (e.g., David) and on and on throughout the Old Testament.

In the New Testament, we start with Mary, a partner to bring Jesus into the world. Jesus came into the world as God's ultimate Partner. Then the disciples and their followers served as His partners in their day and the authors of Scripture in their day to produce Scripture.

Following these there have been countless others, including Luther, Calvin and the other Reformers, followed by the Wesleys, Whitfield, Moody, Billy Graham, right down to us.

Satan Has to Obey the Same Rule

Implied in what I have been saying is the fact that Satan has to obey the same rule. He also needs human partners to accomplish his purposes. And he wins them over through deceit. Thus it was for Adam; Satan deceived him and gained him as a partner. And since he was our father, Adam's sin infected all of us through spiritual inheritance.

Cain partnered with Satan and became the first murderer. The people of Noah's day whom God destroyed because of their wickedness were partnering with Satan. In the book of Exodus we read about a new king, Pharaoh, who came to power and did not abide by the agreement a previous Pharaoh had made with Joseph to protect the nation of Israel. That latter Pharaoh partnered with Satan to persecute the Israelites.

Then we get to the kings of Israel. King Saul started out partnering with God, then switched. Then in the Divided Kingdom, each of the kings of Israel and Judah is evaluated according to what he did with the shrines and high places. All of the kings of Israel and some of the kings of Judah partnered with Satan.

In the New Testament, we see King Herod partnering with Satan to kill Jesus as a baby. Then Satan tried to enlist Jesus as his partner with the temptations (see Luke 4:6–7). The Pharisees partnered with Satan to oppose Jesus, followed by Pilate and the Romans who took Jesus to trial and then killed Him and many of the early Christians.

More recently, we see evil rulers such as Hitler, Stalin, Mao and many others partnering with Satan, plus all who have served Satan down to our day.

And There Seems to Be Another Rule

There is one more rule, which we noted earlier. This rule says: *God will defeat Satan through us, His people.* He will "crush Satan under your feet" (Romans 16:20). Though this is a big assignment, we are dignified by being chosen to be a part of God's army.

A major part of the warfare between God and Satan takes place in the human arena. It is as though *the war is between God's partners and Satan's partners*. This is likely what was behind Satan's tempting of Adam and Eve. God seems to want to prove to Satan that He will defeat him and his human cohorts with our assistance. We are told that God will crush the enemy under *our* feet. This is truly amazing. We might think that God should have known better!

My suspicion, as I have noted, is that God created us and put us in what had been Satan's domain. Perhaps before God created us, Lucifer had been in charge of the entire universe. But then God gave the world to us, and Satan went to work to try to get it back. And he claimed to have done so in Luke 4:6 when he said to Jesus, "I will give you all this power and all this wealth. . . . It has all been handed over to me, and I can give it to anyone I choose" (GNT). Notice that Jesus did not dispute Satan's claim.

So, we live in enemy territory as God's partners, charged to work with God to take back what God once gave to us.

What Does This Mean for Us?

This has ramifications for us. For one thing, since we live behind enemy lines, we are partners in a real war, and we are a real threat to the enemy. It looks as though God depends on us to pull our side of the yoke. He calls us and commissions us to partner with Him to defeat the enemy. There are a number of things in this world that God wants to do with us in His yoke.

He wants to win people to Christ and to free them from the evil one. But He seldom, if ever, does it alone. How often people have asked, "If God wants to convert the heathens or heal and free people, why doesn't He do it by Himself?" He simply does not. Instead, He commands us, "Go into all the world," partnering with Him to win them and initiate them (through baptism) into His forever family, and to bring them freedom in Christ (see Galatians

5:1). God empowers us and sends us out to partner with Him to bring about His Kingdom on earth as in heaven by:

1. Winning the lost through witness—He seldom wins people alone (see Acts 1:8).
2. Healing people—He usually does not heal alone (see Luke 9:1; John 14:12).
3. Casting out demons—He does not free people from demons alone (see Luke 9:1; John 14:12).
4. Teaching under the guidance of the Holy Spirit—He works with partners to teach (see Matthew 28:20).

Our job, then, is to work with God as His partners, to accept the honor of putting on His yoke to enable Him to do what He wants to do. If we do not do our part, God's will does not get done. There is no fatalism in God's program. The mistranslation of Romans 8:28—"all things work together for good"—misrepresents how God has set things up. A better rendering is, "In all things God works together with those who love Him, for their good." Things that God wants to happen do not just automatically happen. They happen when His people do their part by working with Him as partners. Again, the Kingdom of God is *our Kingdom as well as His.*

But will God get His way in the end? Yes, He wins. We see in the book of Revelation that God wins. But we win *with* Him. *He does not win without us.* Though we are the weaker, the apprentice ox, we get to participate in bringing about the Kingdom. It does not happen without us.

We are God's partners. God takes this fact seriously, trusting us to hold up our end. If things go badly, it is usually because we are not doing our part. When we do our part, things go well.

Once more, the Kingdom is *ours* as well as His. I believe this is what He had in mind for Adam—that Adam and his descendants would rule in partnership with God. Jesus, God's ideal Partner, has demonstrated what living a Kingdom life is like—living in total obedience to the Father, partnering with the Father, being guided and empowered by the Holy Spirit, in the yoke as the weaker ox but sharing with God in bringing in the Kingdom. We partner with God to answer Jesus' prayer that God's Kingdom come, that His will be done on earth as it is in heaven (see Matthew 6:10).

That is your true identity.

Do you know who you are?

EXERCISE

Review the exercises you have done thus far. Pick out the most difficult ones and do them now, recognizing how these exercises feed into your life, making you a stronger partner with Jesus.

17

Thoughts and Beliefs

Some questions:

What do you think of yourself?
What does God think of you?
What do others think of you?
What does Satan think of you?

These are critical questions lurking behind the issues we have been dealing with. Does your self-image square with God's view of you? Or are you down on yourself? Let's bring these questions into the light. We have talked about some of these topics, so take a moment with each to evaluate your progress.

What Do You Think of Yourself?

Give an honest answer to this question: What do you think of yourself? Does the fact that you are made in God's image resonate with you? Or is it just another scriptural truth that you cannot seem to get hold of?

I have told you a bit of my story. My reality was formed more by my feeling that I was not worth very much than by the truth that I am really God's masterpiece. Now, having lived a successful life into my eighties, I can accept that truth firmly in my head. But like everyone else, I still face attacks in the war with Satan. He has not stopped looking for weak points in my emotions, wanting me to drift back into feeling unlucky, unwanted, as if my life was a mistake. Now that I know to recognize this for the lie it is, I do not stay there long.

Skirmishes will come in this battle, but you have tools in place to hold steady.

What do you think of yourself?

What Does God Think of You?

Do you ever wonder what God thinks of you? When I greet one of my daughters, I am fond of saying, "You're one of my favorite daughters." (I have two.) Likewise with the boys. "You're one of my favorite sons," I say. (I have two of them also). Four grown children and each one is my favorite. I am proud of them for who they are and for the privilege that is mine to have them in our family.

I try to give them freedom to be themselves, to express themselves in their unique ways. They often ask my advice, and I am usually quick to offer it. They then make their own decisions—and I may or may not agree with what they decide. But even when I disagree, they are still my favorites, and they usually make me proud of them and how they use their free will.

And then come the new generations, brand-new beings who have not existed before. Kids in their parents' image, kids that liven up our lives, kids that make us proud. I sat there with tears in my eyes at our latest family gathering as the youngsters played with each other and with the toys in our toy box! What a blessing to kind of grow up with them again as they grow and learn. Some of them took their first steps in our living room. One of our great-granddaughters lives next door to us and comes to see us daily. We miss her if a day goes by without one of her hugs. She is one of our favorite great-granddaughters.

This, I believe, is how God looks at you and me. We liven up His world and bring Him joy. Our Creator is proud of us, and He is thrilled when we put into practice what we have learned. Not that we never make mistakes. But each one of us is special. Each one of us is His favorite. Each one of us has free will of expression in each unique way—and when that way runs counter to His will, He still loves each one perfectly.

Have you changed in your understanding of what God thinks of you?

What Do Others Think of You?

Our self-image is based largely on our perception of what others think of us. Note that it is *our perception* of what others think. This perception may be way wide of the mark. Or it could be right on the money.

Do your friends see you as mature and self-assured? Or do they see you as immature and weak? Are you secure "in your own skin" or insecure? Maybe you find it hard to love yourself because you perceive others as being critical of you. *How can you be a favorite of God when you feel that even your friends do not think very highly of you?*

The truth is that whatever those around you think of you, you are loved and cherished by the God of the universe. You are God's favorite either way. He has not forgotten you, no matter what others say about you. What they say may have nothing to do with who you really are. What they think is their problem, not yours. You are God's favorite no matter what.

Are you helped or hindered by what others think of you?

What Does Satan Think of You?

Satan knows your true identity and devotes his resources to keeping you from finding out. He knows that you are God's partner and uses every device at his disposal to nullify your understanding of what God wants you to be. A list of his devices would include:

- Keeping you ignorant of his schemes
- Piggybacking on reactions such as fear, anger, shame, rejection, guilt
- Taking advantage of subconscious habits
- Giving life to inherited and contemporary curses
- Keeping alive old insecurities
- Empowering a desire for revenge
- Keeping negative memories alive

In spite of the prominence of the warfare theme in Scripture, the enemy likes to keep our focus off the war. It is probably safe to estimate that in at least eighty to ninety percent of evangelical churches there are no sermons on spiritual warfare. Nor are there deliverances from demons or teaching on how to confront demons.

We claim to want to imitate Jesus but leave out the whole spiritual warfare part that was so prominent in His ministry. We often contend that we are not gifted, or we focus on other parts of the Gospel and sort of assume that Jesus got rid of the demons. We neglect this area as if it does not exist. And Satan and his demons go about their business without hindrance.

That demon who asked me "Where did you get this power?" knew there was power involved—and it was not his. When I told him that it was not mine, but came from Jesus, he knew what I was talking about. He knew that the power was a part of who we are. We carry Jesus' authority and power.

This demon knew this, *but may have never met a human who knew it and could challenge him in the exercise of this power.*

Satan knows who you are. Do you?

Belief and Behavior

What do you know about who you are?

God knows who you are and is waiting for you to find out.

Satan knows who you are and is afraid you might find out.

What about the power and authority God has given you? Does this enter into your belief and behavior? Jesus gave His followers authority and power over all diseases and all demons (see Matthew 28:18–20; Luke 9:1–2). Are you using that power and authority, or are you allowing your enemy to keep you from fighting in the war for freedom?

Many of us are living far below what God expects of us. Are you growing stronger in warfare? Do you feel more confident that you can take a responsible stance?

Jesus knew who He was and set the example for us, challenging the enemy, causing fear on the part of the enemy. He knew where He had come from and where He was going (see John 13:3). With this in mind He knelt down and washed the feet of the disciples, identifying with us just before He took our sins on Himself and paid for our redemption.

Jesus knew who He was (and is); He knew who you were (and are); He knew who the enemy was (and is); and by His free will He took your punishment on Himself. In doing this, He showed His opinion of you, the value He has put on you.

You can lift your head high, knowing what the God of the universe thinks of you.

EXERCISE

Think of times when you have felt free. Go to those times one after another and rejoice. Let yourself feel the freedom. Transition to experiencing what freedom in Jesus must feel like. See how long you can keep that feeling.

18

Doing and Being

Someone has said that we should stop calling ourselves "human beings." The truth is, we are "human doings"! We label ourselves by what we do. If we meet someone, one of the first questions we ask is some variety of the question, "What do you do?" We want to learn the person's occupation so we can have a better understanding of whom we are talking to.

This fact came home to me when someone introduced me once as "an academic." As he said that, I remember feeling *accused*. Though he could have pointed to academic credentials on my part—I have a Ph.D.; I have taught at the postgraduate level for more than fifty years; some 35 books feature my name on the cover—still, when he called me "an academic" (probably to honor me), I felt uncomfortable.

When I got to sit down and ask myself why I felt uncomfortable, I landed on the realization that *academic* is something I do: *Who I am is more. It involves me in a wide variety of different things.* I am more complicated than any of the things I do. I am a man, a husband, a father, a grandfather. I am a Christ-follower, a child of the living God and a bunch of other things. When I do something nice for someone, it is out of the love in my being. Jesus expects us to follow His example. He did what He did because of who He was; we do what we do because of who we are: His followers.

In the Kingdom of God, what we do is to be governed by who we are. We are to do things but not to be defined by those things. People call me a professor, but I am more.

Being Like Jesus

Who we are. This is what this book, and life, is about. We are to be like Jesus and from that base do the things Jesus did. This means being the kind of person that Jesus was.

One of my students, in the quietness of my office, asked me one day, "Do you realize that you put students down when you answer their questions?"

I, of course, denied it.

She simply said, "Watch yourself."

So I did. And she was right.

It hurt to think I might damage students by not listening to them. They mostly asked questions I had heard many times before; I had long since worked out the answers. So I would respond in a way that made me look smart at their expense. My doing held the potential of negatively affecting their being.

I changed. I began to listen all the way through the question, as if I had never heard it before. And I believe I became a better teacher, one truer to my intended being, more like Jesus.

Being like Jesus is not just doing what Jesus did, though it involves doing; doing is the fruit of one's being. Jesus loved and forgave as a lover and forgiver. These were fruits of who He was.

I was ministering to a man who hated his father. As he progressed toward inner healing, he got to the point where he began to understand, accept and forgive his father.

Then he did a very interesting thing. To test whether or not what we did was real, *he tried to hate his father again. And he could not!* He started with *doing* the thing we had worked on (forgiveness) and got to the point where he completely released his father from his resentment and hatred and *became* a forgiver. Forgiveness became a part of his being, a habit.

Which Are You?

Are you "doing" or "being" oriented?

A doing-oriented person slips easily into treating other people as less than fully human beings. Imagine someone operating a piece of machinery. In a sense, the person becomes part of the working mechanism. That operator is using the machine, and the machine is using the operator. It is this same kind of depersonalization that translates to human relationships. People tend to relate to other people essentially as they relate to things—impersonally. We use things and they use us. We use people and they use us.

Think, for example, of how we regard efficiency. We generally assume that it is good to be efficient in whatever we do. We believe we should organize so that any given task will take a minimum of time and energy. We set a time, for instance, for our church services to end—no matter if the subject really needs more time to be developed adequately. We have an efficiency rule that sets aside a certain amount of time for a sermon, and we do not want it to bleed over into the next scheduled event—dinner.

Imagine if during a Sunday sermon someone challenged something the preacher said and started a discussion. People would get uncomfortable because the efficiency rule had been broken, turning a monologue (efficiency event) into a dialogue—a person event. If, on the other hand, a person did the same thing in a small group Bible study meeting without a strict ending time (a person thing), nobody would get upset, for the efficiency rule does not apply (unless the meeting goes too long).

Efficiency, then, is an example of a doing thing. It is a machine thing. Machines are necessary. We can be grateful for them. But if we allow them or any other doing thing to depersonalize us so that we treat people as *things*, we have gone too far.

Satan does not like it when we are people-oriented. He hates people, and anything that helps them is a challenge to his effectiveness. On our side, then, being being-oriented, as Jesus was, is a prerequisite to a healthy self-image. Just as Jesus was person/being-oriented, so we should highly value both others and ourselves, fighting Satan's attempts to diminish our self-image.

EXERCISE

Ponder the distinction between doing and being in your own life. Are you a "human doing"? To the extent that your being is submerged in doing, and that you want to focus more on being, what steps can you take to bring this about?

19

Who We Are in
Three Dimensions

I have found it helpful in understanding Jesus and His expectations in the war with Satan to focus on His life and teachings in three dimensions.[1] These three dimensions are the points at which spiritual warfare is waged. They are allegiance/relationship, truth/knowledge and spiritual power/freedom.

These three crucial dimensions help define who Jesus was and whom He expects us to be. Each covers a good bit of territory, explaining an important part of His and our being. And each highlights areas that characterize redeemed humans and incur Satan's hatred.

Allegiance/Relationship

The first and most important of these dimensions is what I call the *allegiance leading to relationship* dimension.

Jesus put relationship first when He summarized the greatest Commandments: "Love the LORD your God with all your heart, with all your soul, and with all your mind. . . . And . . . love your neighbor as yourself" (Matthew 22:37–39).

The first characteristic of who Jesus was (and whom He wants us to be) is relational, person-oriented, based on allegiance—allegiance on His part issuing in love toward us and toward all humans, His masterpieces.

Jesus taught truth, but as He taught truth He appealed to humans to get into relationship with Him—to pledge allegiance to Him and to grow in that relationship, practicing intimacy with God. He said things like, "I, when I am lifted up from the earth, will draw all people to myself" (John 12:32 ESV) and "Come to me, all of you who are tired from carrying heavy loads" (Matthew 11:28 GNT).

This is the most important of the three dimensions; the other two support it. Picture this dimension of relationship as a tabletop; the aspects of the other dimensions act as legs to hold it up. Without relationship to Jesus, a person is not a Christian, and there is nothing for the other dimensions to support.

Truth/Knowledge

One of the supporting dimensions is *experiential truth and knowledge.* Jesus said, "You shall know the truth, and the truth shall make you free" (John 8:32). He specialized in teaching truth. He even said, "I am the truth" (see John 14:6).

With truth comes knowledge. But He never settled for the intellectualism that has taken over much of our Christianity. He was what we call in our day an activist. He was always out ministering to people, using the tools God had given Him. The use of these tools defined who He was and whom He expects us to be.

Satan stands against truth and freedom; he works overtime to push people to believe inaccurate beliefs and to practice inaccurate practices. An example would be the widespread belief that demons are very powerful in and of themselves. The truth is, while some cosmic-level demons may have what I will label "independent power," the rule for most demons is that there must be something they attach themselves to. This is usually an emotional or spiritual problem, a curse or a dedication.

Believing the lie that demonic power is independent often leads deliverance ministers to fight with demons. What deliverance ministers need to remember is that a demon's power comes from the garbage in which the demon lives. The garbage is the big problem; the demon is the smaller problem. Satan does not want people to know this truth. He wants us to fear and fight demons when they are at their strongest—when they are well attached because the emotional or spiritual garbage that gives them power has not been dealt with.

And there are many other lies as well, all of which affect our being and our doing. Low self-image is one such devastating by-product. We believe his lies; we let Satan win.

But Jesus wants us to hold our heads high as His precious sons and daughters, to know who we are, to fight our enemy and in partnership with Jesus to win.

Spiritual Power/Freedom

The other dimension that supports our relationship to Jesus is *spiritual power leading to freedom*. We need the freedom to respond to the truth we have heard. We can then grow in the saving and freeing relationship we are promised. We are promised that we will become new creatures if we are "in Christ" (2 Corinthians 5:17).

According to Jesus, people, even Christians, are in captivity—not free. So, He came to set captives free (see Luke 4:18–19), to set people free who are hindered in their quest for freedom. He is a "freedom bringer." This is an important part of who He is, His Being. And Satan is not happy when we learn to incorporate freedom-bringing into who we are.

Probably all of us resonate with the loving and forgiving part of who Jesus was when He walked on this earth. Jesus was relationship-oriented. He loved people. We hear a lot of sermons on the love part of Jesus' ministry, and we work to be more like Him in this area. Love and forgiveness are very important; learning to function as lovers and forgivers should be a major part of our growing to be more like Jesus.

But Jesus also said that we are to do the works He did and more (see John 14:12)! This means that healing and deliverance are to be a part of our being. Unfortunately, this part of our quest is widely ignored by Christ-followers, a part of being like Jesus that we tend to skip over. But healing (both physical and emotional) along with deliverance from evil spirits is very important to Jesus.

Jesus offers freedom as well as salvation. And using power to bring freedom is a major part of being a Christ-follower. We are to live in that freedom. But living in freedom as Jesus did also means helping others get free.

Free from what? According to Luke 9:1–2, Jesus wants us to be free and to help others be free from demons and diseases. We need to add the power part of Jesus' (and our) being and doing to the love and forgiveness part. We are His agents to bring freedom from our enemy.

Remember our spiritual credit card: We are not simply to sit back and expect God to run this world. We must partner with Him in healing it and taking it away from the enemy. We are called to be healers—those who love and work in power to free people.[2] *That is who we are, and that is what Satan does not want us to learn.*

These are the three dimensions of who Jesus is—and whom He wants us to be. First, God is a relational God. He is concerned about our relationships to Him, to others and even to ourselves. This dimension is supported by the way Jesus practiced and taught truth and knowledge, by which we gain understanding. It is also supported by Jesus' demonstrations of spiritual power and our position of partnering with Him to take back the earth. And the result for us is freedom.

May God bless you with the discovery of your true identity in both love and power.

Fully Free!

Let's take a moment now, as we draw our study to a close, to celebrate our walk of freedom.

We have surveyed self-image territory on a quest to discover both who we are and who we are supposed to be.

We have considered the relationship between self-image and spiritual warfare and noted that it is a part of Satan's activity to encourage low self-image. He is happiest when we are most down on ourselves. He loves it when we get discouraged and quit. We have learned that we are partners with Jesus, and that God wants us to wield authority and power as we pray for His Kingdom to come.

Our best approach to the low self-image problem is to look squarely at who we are and act with confidence in opposing our enemy. To do this we need to:

1. Fight low self-esteem
2. Experience the truth about who we are
3. Recognize that we are in God's image
4. Remember who we are
5. See ourselves as higher than the angels
6. Recognize that we have been chosen before Creation
7. Know that we have been adopted into God's forever family
8. Know that we will never be abandoned
9. Know that we alone of all creatures have been redeemed
10. Know the dignity of Jesus' choice to be one of us
11. Participate in God's war against Satan
12. Know that we are temples of God
13. Know that God has given us a "credit card"
14. Know the honor of being able to create others in His image
15. Know the joy of being in partnership with God

16. Know the joy of setting captives free
17. Participate with Jesus in defeating Satan
18. Live yoked with Jesus in partnership
19. Recognize that God has given us His power and authority to heal and to cast out demons
20. Allow these truths to transform our view of ourselves
21. Know what God thinks of us and expects of us

What a list! And it may not be complete.

The enemy wants us to feel that we do not have permission to think well of ourselves. "That would be pride," he says, "and pride is not a Christian virtue."

So, we start to agree with him. "A true Christian," we decide, "runs from any smell of seeing himself as good. After all, we are all miserable sinners." We interpret the Bible that way.

The Bible says, "All have sinned" (Romans 3:23) and "the heart is deceitful above all things, and desperately wicked" (Jeremiah 17:9) and "our righteousnesses are as filthy rags" (Isaiah 64:6 KJV). These things are true. But they are not the complete story. Satan has latched onto them and convinced us that they are the whole truth and uses them to put us down and keep us from focusing on the positive things that define who we really are.

We are sinners and disappoint God regularly, just as children sin and disappoint their parents. But that is only part of the story. In spite of children's failures, loving parents will not give up on them. Neither does God give up on us. He has gone so far as to forgive us our disappointments as well as our sins by taking them on Himself.

There is not much we know about how He does it. But we do know that the judgment and condemnation we deserve have been taken away. He has forgiven our "oversteps" and our "understeps"—the times when we have done wrong by doing too much and those times when we have done wrong by not doing enough. *Everything!*

Forgiven, accepted, put back standing on our feet again—that is who we are.

My wife and I were able to pay off our house this year. We are now free and clear from the biggest financial commitment we have ever made. And I cannot tell you how wonderful it feels. Whenever I think about the house, I am overwhelmed by the feeling of *freedom*. There is nothing left that I owe. It belongs to us now, no longer to the bank.

God gives us that kind of freedom on a much grander scale. Our debt is paid and we are free! No more a large monthly bill to pay! Free!

That is who we are.

That is who *you* are.

Walk in your freedom.

EXERCISE

Picture yourself running freely in the breeze, experiencing freedom to the maximum.

Notes

Chapter 2: Satan Is Not Happy about Us

1. For a more in-depth look at this topic, please see my book *Defeating Dark Angels* (Chosen, 2016).

Chapter 8: Redeemed

1. For further help with these topics, please see my books *Two Hours to Freedom* (Chosen, 2010) and *Deep Wounds, Deep Healing* (Chosen, 2014).

Chapter 9: Dignified by the Incarnation

1. Please see *I Give You Authority* (Chosen, 2012).

Chapter 11: Spiritual Warfare

1. For help with imitating Jesus' behavior in this neglected area, you might find my book *The Evangelical's Guide to Spiritual Warfare* (Chosen, 2015) a good place to start.

Chapter 19: Who We Are in Three Dimensions

1. See *The Evangelical's Guide to Spiritual Warfare* pages 105–111 for a different application of this same concept.

2. I have written on this and suggest you read *Two Hours to Freedom* with the aim of learning to be a healer, as Jesus was. If you are shaky about the authority you need to bring freedom, my book *I Give You Authority* will help. The power is there and Jesus delights in your discovering who you are in power as well as love.

Bibliography

Anderson, Neil. *Victory Over the Darkness*. Minneapolis: Bethany, 2014.

Kraft, Charles H. *Deep Wounds, Deep Healing*. Minneapolis: Chosen, 2014.

———. *Defeating Dark Angels*. Minneapolis: Chosen, 2014.

———. *The Evangelical's Guide to Spiritual Warfare*. Minneapolis: Chosen, 2015.

———. *I Give You Authority*. Minneapolis: Chosen, 2012.

———. *Two Hours to Freedom*. Minneapolis: Chosen, 2010.

Schacter, Daniel. *Searching for Memory*. New York: Basic Books, 1996.

Index

Charles H. Kraft is professor emeritus in the School of Intercultural Studies at Fuller Seminary, having taught there for 41 years as professor of anthropology and intercultural communication. He taught anthropology, communication, contextualization and spiritual warfare to missionaries and prospective missionaries.

He holds degrees from Wheaton College (B.A.), Ashland Theological Seminary (B.D.) and Hartford Seminary Foundation (Ph.D.). He served as a missionary in Nigeria and taught linguistics and African languages at Michigan State (five years) and UCLA (five years) before his time at Fuller Seminary.

He is the author of 36 books and numerous articles on African languages, Christianity in culture, intercultural communication, inner healing, spiritual warfare and related fields.

He is married to Dr. Marguerite Kraft, who taught intercultural studies at Biola University for 31 years.

They are parents of four grown children with fifteen grandchildren and fifteen great-grandchildren.

More Powerful Resources from Charles H. Kraft

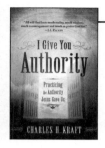

With incredible insight, respected scholar and teacher Dr. Charles Kraft helps awaken you to the extraordinary authority you have been given through the Holy Spirit. Kraft explains what spiritual authority is and isn't, and describes the responsible exercise of such authority in key areas. You have the authority of heaven itself. How will you use it?

I Give You Authority

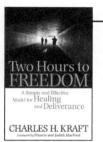

Respected evangelical scholar and missionary Dr. Charles Kraft offers an uncomplicated approach to deep-level inner healing, helping readers identify their problems, receive deliverance and heal the leftover wounds.

Two Hours to Freedom

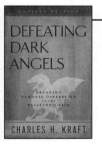

Defeating Dark Angels features firsthand accounts of demonic activity in the lives of "ordinary" people, providing a biblical understanding of why and how dark forces come against God's people. Scholarly research and practicality, for personal deliverance, emotional healing and ministry.

Defeating Dark Angels

You May Also Like . . .

Experience real and lasting freedom from a painful past. Whether you are seeking restoration for yourself or for those under your care, this book will enable you to recognize the spiritual roots of emotional wounds and invite God's presence into those darkest of places.

Deep Wounds, Deep Healing
by Charles H. Kraft with Ellyn Kearney and Mark H. White